SON OF A SANDSTORM

Life and Travels of an Okie Vagabond

Ray Burrus

ISBN 978-1-68526-227-3 (Paperback)
ISBN 978-1-68526-228-0 (Digital)

First Edition

Covenant Books, Inc.
11661 Hwy 707
Murrells Inlet, SC 29576
www.covenantbooks.com

CONTENTS

PREFACE

Life has been eventful for me, Raymond Burrus. I have been a sales executive, an international entrepreneur, a vagabond in Europe and Africa, an army officer, an entertainer, a college and master's track-and-field athlete, a fraternity brother, a Christian, a father, a grandfather, husband, brother, and son.

Most of the experiences in this book took place before I was twenty-seven. By that time, I had grown up in Oklahoma; attended a major university on a track scholarship; served in the US Army four years, coming home from Vietnam a captain; traveled in over fifty countries, including vagabonding overland the length of Africa. During those ten adult years before age twenty-seven, I kept a journal much of the time and recorded my thoughts and experiences.

This book took root as a progressive letter-writing exercise when my oldest daughter, Elizabeth, went away to the University of Texas in 1995. I knew I would miss her, and so I suggested that I write her every week to stay in touch.

So with her agreement, I decided to write my life story in two-to-three-page weekly letters. This continued for a total of eighty letters spread over her college career. I also gave each of the letters to my other daughter Katherine so she would have the same story from me.

As the letters developed over time, I also shared them with other people, who suggested I write a book. It's been twenty-six years since Elizabeth went away to college, and the letters sat in a drawer waiting to be shared. Unfortunately, life got in the way, and I found myself working to make a living, changing jobs several times; time raced by. I now find myself retired and with no more excuses for why I haven't written the book. My mother, Dorothy Burrus, who is now 102 years old, has encouraged me to finish it.

So what follows is the story of my younger days. Before I begin, I must acknowledge the great debt I owe to the woman who has shared these last forty-eight years with me: my wife, Susan. She has suffered through hearing these stories so many times with tolerance beyond measure. Without her love and devotion, this book would not have been possible.

CHAPTER 1

MY YOUTH AND CHILDHOOD

You dragged your bike under a train?

As a child, I had a level of independence unheard of today. We lived in five different towns in Oklahoma until we finally moved to Stillwater, where I attended both high school and college. I remember in second grade (age seven), my mother went back to work, and after she left, taking my five-year old sister with her, I had to wait until it was time to go to school and then ride my bike eight or ten blocks to the elementary school. One day, I encountered a problem: a train parked on the tracks, blocking my route to school. So what to do? I was not allowed to go another route—busy streets. I couldn't be late to school, so I did the only logical thing: I dragged my bike under the train and went on to school. Returning home after school and relating this innovative solution to my mom, I was made to understand that was not a good idea (they called it a *spanking* back then).

When I was five, we lived with my grandmother Jones. She was this wonderfully loving little rotund lady, who had a saying for everything. When I worried about how others thought of me, she'd say, "Raymond, you wouldn't worry about what others thought of you if you knew how seldom they did!" Everything she touched tasted good, so we never had a bad meal at her house. She drove a huge Pontiac station wagon around the little village of Mingo, just northeast of Tulsa.

Once, on the way home from church, Granddaddy stopped at a little gas station. When I went to exit the back seat, Granddaddy slammed the front door with my hand in it. He took me aside and poured raw kerosene on my bleeding hand and told me to get back in the car. Tough love!

When we lived in the small town of Guthrie and I was eight, Saturday mornings were a time we all looked forward to. My mother would give me a quarter. I would meet my friends from the Masonic Children's Home, and we would walk the eight or ten blocks to the movies downtown. I would buy a ticket to the movie (ten cents), a Coke (ten cents), and a PayDay candy bar (five cents), and that was it for Saturday mornings.

It was also in this small town that my dad took me to a football game, and at halftime, they had footraces for the kids. I remember vividly the hair standing up on the back of my neck watching the competition and the thrill I felt winning my first footrace—barefoot, of course.

When we moved from Guthrie to Oklahoma City, it was a big deal to our family because Dad was moving from a kind of ho-hum job to a political appointment where he would have an office in the Oklahoma Capitol Building. His job was executive director of the Oklahoma Soil Conservation Service. It was a jump to a position of some prominence in state government circles. We bought a house exactly one block north of the Oklahoma governor's mansion and three blocks east of the capitol in a nice middle-class neighborhood.

But before we moved, I was allowed to go to West Texas to spend the summer with my granddaddy Burrus. It was my first experience away from home. The prospect of getting to spend the whole summer out there was for me like getting to go to a do-it-yourself summer camp. Granddaddy let me help him milk the cows; he always had four to six cows, and he had names for all of them, and it seemed that they knew their names when he spoke to them. He also had chickens and pigs that needed feeding and tending, and I got to go collect the eggs and slop the hogs every day. He got water from a windmill, which stood out by the barn, that pumped the most foul-tasting water up from somewhere deep in the ground. The only way I could drink it was in heavily sweetened ice tea.

I'd like to describe my granddaddy Decatur Burrus for you, but I just don't know if I can do it justice. He was about five feet ten inches tall, and he always wore overalls and smelled of fresh tobacco. He carried a pouch of tobacco in the chest pocket of his overalls with some papers, and he rolled his own cigarettes. My dad said that when Granddaddy Burrus was younger, he could roll a cigarette in his pocket while riding a horse in a blowing sandstorm.

I never saw him shave, but he always seemed to have about a three-day growth of stubble on his chin. When he was older and someone mentioned retirement, he would say, "Not for me. We rust out. We don't wear out." In other words, stay active your whole life, and you'll live longer and better. He had a pleasant, comforting countenance. I never heard him raise his voice in anger, and he always had a gentleness about him that a child really understands. I loved being near him.

Life in 1954 in West Texas was very basic. No TV yet, and for that matter, they had only had electricity about ten years and indoor plumbing about five. When they told Granddaddy Burrus about the indoor plumbing, he thought for a minute and said, "Why, that's just not something you do in the house!"

He would wake me at dawn, with him sitting in the dark, listening to the farm report on the radio. I would jump up and follow him out to the barn, where the cows would be waiting with full udders to be milked—no machines, he milked them every day of his life by hand and carried the milk into the kitchen, where he put it in the separator. The separator spun the milk around, and the heavier cream was separated from the milk. We would have fresh milk, fresh bacon from his own pigs, fresh eggs from his chickens, and homemade biscuits. It was a very simple, self-sufficient life and a land of enchantment for an eight-year-old kid from Oklahoma.

Summer days were filled with hoeing weeds in the cotton fields and sometimes visiting my cousins Gayle and Marsha on the next farm. Uncle Tom taught me to drive his pickup, and I did fine until I tried backing up.

It was a great and memorable summer for me. At the end of the summer, Granddaddy took me (reluctantly) to Lubbock and put me on an American Airlines plane back to Oklahoma City—my first plane ride! This was1954; no jets yet, and for an eight-year-old, it was very exciting. But when it was time to go, there was a problem:

My sister JoBeth left a doll in West Texas, and Mom asked me to bring it back. Carry a doll? No way! The compromise was that I would carry it wrapped up in brown paper so no one would see that it was a doll. I remember getting off that plane in Oklahoma City, coming down the steps (no Jetways), and getting rid of that doll to JoBeth as quickly as possible!

Even when we moved to Oklahoma City, I had lots of freedom. I remember riding my bike to Dewey School down a long hill about ten blocks long. If we really cranked our bikes, we could go fast enough to make it up the hill at the end to the school without much effort. The problem was, there was a stop sign halfway down on Thirtieth. If we stopped, we couldn't make it up the hill to school without pedaling hard. Solution? Blow right through the stop sign, making ourselves a smaller target.

Our family attended Trinity Baptist Church, where there was a very active and fun youth group. I joined the youth choir, and we would be back at church every Sunday at 4:00 p.m. for choir practice. We rehearsed a music piece in four-part harmony and sang it during evening church. I was placed in the tenor section and stood next to an older guy who could read music. He would point to the notes we sang, and that's how I learned to read music. I really loved being part of that choir, singing beautiful music in four-part harmony.

I also played basketball for Trinity in the church leagues for several years. At that time, many of the churches in Oklahoma City had gyms, and the basketball games were very competitive.

I attended Northeast for junior high, a school that went from seventh to twelfth grade. It was 1958, and some of the guys who quit school to fight in Korea were back to finish high school. So as an eleven-year-old, I was attending school with guys who were twenty and twenty-one. It was a tough school, and I remember seeing pistols pulled out of coat pockets. The new kids were threatened with being pantsed; the bigger kids would take the pants off the younger ones and run them up the flagpole. They never caught me, but some others were humiliated.

Summer of the eighth grade, my friend Buddy and I decided to start a bike repair shop in his garage. Kids from the neighborhood would bring their bikes for painting, gluing flame stickers on the sides, and tune-ups. I don't remember if we made any money, but I do remember one incident clearly: I was testing a bike around the block when, going too fast, I hit the curb and went over the handlebars onto the pavement. When I picked up the bike, my arms bent about two inches above the wrists—oops, this isn't right. I had broken both bones in both arms—two casts on my arms and a lost baseball season. Mom put plastic bags on my arms so I could play in the creek during our summer camping trip—had to do that.

As a ninth grader, I was told by some seniors that it was a dangerous place, and if I surrendered my lunch money, they could take care of me. I basically told them to get stuffed because I was pretty sure I could outrun them if necessary, but most of my classmates gave up the money. Later, when they were found out and expelled, I was almost implicated because I had refused to give up the money, and the teachers thought I must be involved.

Another thing I remember from that year was the integration of our school. I think it was one of the first schools in Oklahoma to be integrated, so they brought a few scholar-athletes up from the black school Douglas High to prove it would work. Of course, there was some tension. One guy—Herman, a year younger than me—played the same position in football as me, so we saw a lot of each other and became friends. Our games were on Thursdays, and our coach would line Herman and me up and make us run a forty-yard dash, and the winner would start the next game. I started some, and so did he. There were a couple of times when older kids would say terrible things to Herman in my presence. I wanted to confront them and maybe fight it out, but he always said, "No! Just ignore them."

Summer after my ninth-grade year, I joined a Boy Scout adventure trip, canoeing up into the Boundary Waters of Northern Minnesota and the Canadian Quetico Provincial Park. This was my first big trip away from my folks, and it opened a whole new world for me. Two of my pals—Jimmy and Flip—and I, who were athletes, were recruited to go on the trip (I think the scoutmaster just wanted to make sure he wouldn't have to do all the heavy lifting). We paddled ninety miles up into Canada over three weeks, and I got my first taste of adventure travel, which would later consume me.

Another life-changing thing happened that ninth-grade year. There were fifty guys trying out for basketball, and that put me off. A new guy at our school and I were horsing around in gym class, and as a wrestler, he saw some potential in me. So I went out for wrestling. I only weighed 120 pounds, soaking wet, and was small for my age. I feared the bigger older kids, but when I learned how to wrestle to take someone down and neutralize them, it changed everything for me. I gained a new self-image and no longer feared the "tough guys."

In the spring of 1961, after John Kennedy was elected, my father got appointed to be the executive director of the ASCS, the top federal agricultural job in Oklahoma, which meant a move to Stillwater. As it happened, the guy who convinced me to go out for wrestling had moved from Stillwater the year before, so he accompanied me on a trip to introduce me to his pals. It was a great introduction and made the move easy for me.

So at the end of that summer of 1961, our family moved to Stillwater, a small town of about thirteen thousand, mostly rural and agricultural, certainly not the cosmopolitan life of Oklahoma City. Not a good fit for me, and I really missed the friends I had grown up with. I was able to hook up with a baseball team, Jim Smith Café Team, fourteen and under league. That gave me a first sports connection in Stillwater and, since I could play first base well, a leg up.

Since Stillwater is a college town, the high school kids all think they are preparing or already college ready, and so I was thrown into a more grown-up environment than my cocoon of friends in OKC. Lots of drinking and smoking even among fifteen-year-olds, which put me off. At that time in my life, Christianity was a central focus for me, and I made friends easily at the First Baptist Church.

I met a girl there, and it was my first real relationship. Barbara and I spent a lot of time together that first year and attended Bible studies together. At one of those meetings, I objected to something the pastor said, and he chastised me for questioning him, embarrassing me in front of my friends. I went home and told my parents I was finished with that church. They insisted that I go somewhere to worship each week, so by myself, I joined another church and continued to attend there all through the rest of high school and college.

All my time in high school, I felt like an outsider. There was a culture of athletics being so important that other activities were clearly lower in popularity. I was active in sports but didn't want to only be defined by that. I could sing tenor and read music, and back in Oklahoma City, I was also interested in acting, but those things went by the wayside as I dedicated all my energies to sports—and girls, of course. I took the hardest courses and associated with the math and science geeks to be different. But my status as a leader in sports put me on the outside of that group.

My summer jobs were mostly hard labor: At fifteen, I worked at the Stillwater Feed Mill, hoisting one-hundred-pound sacks of feed all day for fifty cents an hour, ten hours a day.

The next summer, I worked for a construction company hammering nails and pouring concrete all day. Two summers, my friend Roger and I sold firecrackers. We set up stands on all four corners of town and hired our girlfriends to work for us. It was our first entrepreneurial experience, and we made good money during the Fourth of July.

My last year of high school, I took the hardest courses available and got more serious about academics. I have spoken with many people who applied to several colleges before deciding on the best one for them. That never occurred to me. I just always assumed I'd go to Oklahoma State University on a track scholarship. Both my parents had gone there, and my dad ran track.

However, I didn't get a scholarship offer until about sixty days before we started college. I was invited to run in an invitational meet of champions track meet in Tulsa, and I won the high hurdles in that meet with the OSU coach present. He offered me a half scholarship on the spot.

I attended OSU from 1964 until 1968, dividing my time between academics, the fraternity I joined (Beta Theta Pi), and athletics. I renewed my love of singing and joined the OSU Men's Glee Club, and we performed all over, including a trip to Colorado

Springs. Track guys were out of town at meets almost every weekend of the spring semester so we couldn't take more than twelve to fourteen hours of classwork. So in the fall semesters, we had to double up with sixteen to eighteen hours if we expected to graduate in four years. I also took summer school two of those years to catch up.

A major issue hanging over the heads of all male students was the draft. The Vietnam War was going on, and none of us wanted to be drafted. We had a 2-S deferment for being in college, which meant that we would not be drafted if we were in school. At that time, since OSU was a land-grant school, all male freshmen and sophomores were required to enroll in military science and be part of the ROTC program.

At the end of my sophomore year, the Big Eight outdoor track meet was in Lawrence, Kansas, and I got third in my event, scoring for the team. When we returned to school, I asked for a full scholarship since I had contributed to our team score. He refused, and I insisted, threatening to quit if I didn't get the full ride. And at this point, I learned a life lesson: never threaten to do something without considering all the consequences. The coach looked at me and said, "Clean out your locker!" So I lost my track scholarship.

Now what? The army was short on midlevel officers because so many guys just did their two years and got out. So they were offering a scholarship similar to the track scholarship, which would obligate us for four years active duty, so I applied. There were nine scholarships over a five-state area, and after impressing a board of senior officers, I got one. I assumed that I would have to serve in the military, and going in as an officer would give me some control over my destiny. The scholarships, which provided all school expenses and one hundred dollars per month, filled a need for me and was a lot of money in 1966.

That summer of 1966, when I was twenty, I went to work for the Southwestern Bible Company. After a week of training in Nashville, our crew came to central Texas, where we were each assigned a county to work. I was assigned to Hill County, where I lived in an old hotel in downtown Hillsboro. The books I sold were a Layman's Bible Library with a Bible reference book, a children's Bible storybook, and a Bible concordance.

It was a tough summer. I had never done door-to-door selling before and never lived away from home alone. There were supposed to be two of us living and supporting each other, but the other guy quit after a couple of weeks, so I was left alone. For every customer who was interested, there were twelve to fifteen customers who either slammed the door in my face or just weren't interested. It was hard not to get discouraged with all that rejection.

I learned a lot about selling, the most important of which was the law of averages. There is a certainty that if you have a good product that people want, then people will buy. If you know that every twelfth or fifteenth presentation, someone will buy, then it's easy arithmetic: every *no* gets you closer to a *yes*. So when I learned to look at it that way, I began to get serious about making calls, and my attitude improved.

I averaged working seventy-five hours a week that summer, making fourteen to fifteen sales calls every day, six days a week. I brought home about 1,200 dollars that summer and won a new suit and pair of wing tips from the company. At the end of the summer, I delivered the books I sold, collected the money, and returned home.

It was a good summer for me. Living alone in a hotel in downtown Hillsboro, working twelve-hour days, catching meals when I could squeeze them in—it was a tough make-or-break situation. I got a call from a sales manager in Nashville every week, and he told me to put a reminder up on my bathroom mirror that said, "I feel happy. I feel healthy. I feel terrific." The power of positive thinking!

But it wasn't all work. I met the daughter of the preacher at the First Baptist Church the first week I was there. She made sure I had a good meal at least once a week and a little social life in the evenings. We spent a lot of time together that summer, going on dates, skinny dipping in the lake, and enjoying what little time I took off.

I met a lot of nice people that summer. On many sales calls out in the country with houses spaced a half mile apart, after knocking on the screen door, I would hear, "Come on in. We're back in the kitchen."

I would say, "You'd better come out here and have a look at me first. I'm a stranger."

Then they would usually say, "Aw, come on in here, boy. You hungry?" That was Central Texas in 1966—friendly people, salt of the earth.

That summer demonstrated to me the concept of success as it relates to persistence. It also showed me in a very tangible way that people are generally nice folks everywhere you go. If you just extend a hand of friendship, you'll get the same in return. This was demonstrated for me in much more graphic detail when I would go on my year-and-a-half odyssey through Europe and Africa.

The last two years of college were very rewarding for me. I got involved in campus politics and served in the student senate. I also was elected senior class president, captain of the track team, and voted a top-ten senior in the university. I graduated top of my class with a degree in business management and received my second lieutenant bars the same day. During this last year of school, I realized my life as a track athlete was coming to an end, and I got disillusioned with religion. So for the next twenty years, I left Christianity. I still believed in God, but it was the late '60s and '70s, a time of "if it feels good, do it," and I did.

I put everything I owned in my little Buick Skylark and left Stillwater, looking in the rearview mirror at my mom waving goodbye. A week later, I was on active duty as a Transportation Corps officer at Fort Eustis, Virginia, with orders to report for my first duty assignment in Germany after six weeks of officer basic training.

CHAPTER 2

TMO Nuremburg

"Colonel Dorman, Sergeant Lentz wants to talk to you."

In my first week in command, the sergeant in charge walked boldly into my office and asked which magazines I liked. I told him, and he said he'd get them for me and for me to just stay in my office reading my magazines, and he'd run this place the way it ought to be run. I asked him who would sign all the documents. He told me I would, and I explained that if I was to be signing the documents, then I needed to be in charge and run the place.

An argument ensued, so I picked up the phone and called the colonel in Frankfurt, to whom I reported. I said, "Colonel Dorman, Sergeant Lentz wants to talk to you." At this, the sergeant started waving his arms, saying he really *didn't* want to talk to the colonel. It worked. I made it clear to him that "officer in charge" meant that I was happy to work with him but on my terms. Whatever I could delegate to him, I would, but I was in charge. I grew up that day.

I left Stillwater, Oklahoma, in August of 1968, driving east to Fort Eustis, Virginia, home of the US Army Transportation Corps. Because of my army scholarship, I got to choose my branch and first duty assignment as a priority. I chose transportation and Germany, hoping that the Vietnam War would be over before I finished my time in Germany. It wasn't.

This was my first adult experience. College and my childhood home disappeared in the rearview mirror as I excitedly reported for duty. The first two months were in an officer basic course, teaching us the ins and outs of moving people and things around the world efficiently. We also had to qualify physically, but for me, that was the easy part.

From the beginning, I rebelled against the military; the saluting, antiquated military courtesy, and infinite rules and bureaucracy distressed me, and I spent the whole four years pushing back against it. But I also learned that you don't take the army on directly; it was too big and powerful an organization to buck or change, so I just had to work around all that and do the best I could. In retrospect, I can see now that having a uniform to wear and not having to choose a wardrobe, having a clear position in the pecking order with some influence and leadership, I had it pretty good.

Even though I was an unwilling participant and had no interest in making it a career, I resolved to do the best I could under the circumstances so that I could look back on a job well done. That meant working around the system to get things done, but as I soon learned, that's the way everyone operates in the army.

My first duty station was Frankfurt, Germany, home of the Transportation Command, Europe. This was my first transcontinental plane ride and only my second jet plane ride ever. I arrived in the morning and was picked up by another officer in the unit, was dropped off at the bachelor officers' quarters, and told to report across the street on Monday morning.

Knowing nothing about jet lag, I promptly took a nap, awakening in late afternoon wide awake and hungry. I walked outside in the bleak, cold October Frankfurt evening and realized that I didn't know where I was, I didn't have any local money, I didn't speak the language, I didn't know anyone there, and I was completely alone. I was hungry but didn't know where a restaurant was, what they ate there, or even how to order food. I've never felt so lonely and forlorn in my life before or since.

I spent a few weeks in Frankfurt and then went to my permanent duty station in Nuremburg. It was a major's position, but all the captains and majors were off fighting in Vietnam, so as a brand-new butter-bar lieutenant, I assumed the duties of transportation movements officer (TMO) for North Bavaria. I was totally clueless, but with the arrogance and exuberance of youth, I was able to succeed.

It wasn't without incident, though. The office had three main functions: to coordinate truck movements of military material in and out of North Bavaria, to coordinate convoy movements into and out of the training areas, and coordinate movement of heavy equipment on the railroad into and out of North Bavaria. I decided that I would run the office using management lessons I had learned at OSU: that even though these guys were draftees, their desire was to do the best job they could. I believed that if I could empower them with the right training and the right motivation and get out of the way, they would do a great job for me. They didn't need a lot of inspections, haircuts, and military harassment; what they needed was someone who believed in them and supported them. Of course, the noncoms resisted this approach, but when they saw it working and when we collaborated on it, they eventually came along.

We developed a reputation for being one of the most efficient, error-free offices in the system with little to no disciplinary problems. I had to communicate with my boss once a month with a written narrative of what we accomplished each month, and because I was a creative writer, they seemed satisfied and left us alone.

What that meant for me personally was that it became pretty much an eight-to-five job with every weekend free. The schoolteachers and nurses had officer's club privileges, so it was a hopping place, and those thirty months were a great time for me. I got promoted to first lieutenant and captain on the first and second anniversaries of my service, and life was very good.

I hadn't been in the job very long when the army had a big exercise called Reforger. It involved an entire division of men. They lived in Kansas but also had equipment and supplies in storage in Germany. The exercise involved getting them over to Germany, pick up their equipment, travel to the training area in North Bavaria, and then fly back from Nuremburg. My responsibility was to set up the train cars for their equipment and assign convoy clearance orders for them to travel overland to the training area and finally to get them all back to the airport. Then I was to attend the training in a support role.

We were sitting in a Quonset hut around a stove during that snowy January exercise, trying to keep warm, when the door blew open and a general blew in. He stomped over to my desk with a few field grade officers in tow and asked who oversaw transportation. When I stood up and told him it was me, he said, "Let me make something perfectly clear, lieutenant: this operation will not fail because of ground transportation. Do you understand?"

In the silence that followed, and we heard the winter storm howling outside, one of my sergeants, Jerry Crawford, to whom I will always be in debt, stepped in front of me and asked if we could act on his authority to make sure there were no delays. The general nodded and stomped back out into the blizzard. My sergeant looked over at me and winked. He was married to a German girl, and his brother-in-law owned a fleet of luxury Mercedes buses that would go anywhere in any conditions.

We called the brother-in-law and set up around the clock transport to get all twelve thousand troops back to the Nuremburg Airport during the blizzard, on time for all their flights back to Kansas. When the bill for chartering the buses hit the colonel's desk, I got a quick angry phone call. I asked the colonel to check with the general before he court-martialed me, and when he did, he was totally surprised. Both the sergeant and I got Army Commendation Medals for that exercise.

That first year in Nuremburg, I got word that my grandfather had died back in Oklahoma. I called my boss in Frankfurt and told him I wanted to go to the funeral. He explained that if it was a member of my immediate family, he could cut orders for me to fly back for free. He said, "So did you say your father died?" Naively, I told him it was my grandfather, and he said, "Listen to me, son. Did you say your father died?"

I kept that job for thirty-two months. I got my guys good accommodation or possibly some extra money to live off post with their girlfriends. I got them promoted as soon as I could, and they in turn performed admirably the whole time. Of course, there were some misfits; that was inevitable in an army of conscription. Sergeant Crawford had to "help a few boys down the stairs" occasionally. But by and large, we dealt with the problems and were commended for our good work.

Because I reported to someone in Frankfurt and lived in Nuremburg, I had no responsibilities for the mundane work most young officers must do, which left me free to enjoy my off-duty time. At the officer's club, the young officers gathered and met either schoolteachers or nurses (there was a large school complex and a major hospital complex in Nuremburg). It wasn't long before I met several new friends. Remember, it was the late '60s and early '70s, so the "if it feels good, do it" attitude was running strong.

I had never been skiing, and since I was existing on 280 dollars a month, it was hard to learn to ski, but one of my nurse friends was a big girl, and her boots and skis fit me, so I would ride down to Austria with her and other friends and learned to ski on her old equipment. I said, "What do I do?"

She said, "Just point your toes and come on down!"

I did, picked it up quickly, and loved it. By the third year there, I owned all my own ski equipment and was getting in twelve to thirteen ski weekends a year.

In the summer of 1969, my girlfriend from college days Susan Scheffel came over to Germany to see me. I helped her get a place for the summer with some schoolteacher friends of mine, and we enjoyed North Bavaria and several trips around Europe. During that summer, my parents made their first trip to Europe, and the four of us took a two-week trip together.

We drove down through Austria to Italy, back up along the French Riviera and up to Paris, then through Belgium, Holland, and over to England. By the time we got to England, my poor dad, who was making his first trip to Europe, had seen six or seven countries, all with different currencies and was totally confused as to what was worth what. In those days, the English penny was as large as a silver dollar and called a *copper*. We had taken a taxi downtown to see a play in London, and as I was helping Susan and my mom out of the taxi, I asked dad to pay the guy. He reached in his pocket, and seeing the large copper coins, he stuck his hand in the window of the taxi and said, "There you go, boy. Take a handful of them biguns." I intervened and told him the driver wanted folding money.

When we got back to Nuremburg, Susan had to decide what to do next. She had enjoyed her summer in Germany and decided to see if she could get a job and stay. After WWII, the Army Corps of Engineers had run copper telephone wire between all the bases, so we had our own private phone system. She got on my office phone and started phoning the schools at bases around Europe to see if they needed teachers. In no time, she found a school in Frankfurt that needed a third-grade teacher, and she was sworn in as a GS-9 teacher in the Department of Defense School System. She taught in Frankfurt for two years, about 150 miles from Nuremburg, and we saw each other occasionally over the next few years. I knew in my heart that I wanted her to be in my life but just couldn't figure out how just yet. We both had more single living to do.

In the summer of 1970, all the other officers with whom I had arrived in Europe in the army were being promoted to captain and getting orders to go to Vietnam. I was in Nuremburg, finishing up two years there, with everyone else receiving orders for captain and Vietnam at the same time, and the army had not sent me anything. I was told I would stay in Europe another year and then spend my last year in a short-term assignment (read Vietnam).

I had my job under control, and I was bored. So I volunteered for "jump school," airborne training. Being a parachutist in the army was more than just another skill to learn or another badge to wear on the uniform. People who are airborne-qualified are a club unto themselves. If you weren't airborne, you were just a *leg*. It was known as very rigorous training, which a lot of guys didn't finish because of either the physical or mental pressure they put you under, a challenge I couldn't resist! So I volunteered, even though there was a distinct possibility that I would be immediately reassigned to an airborne unit in Vietnam. The fact that I still went says a lot about how bored I was in Nuremburg.

I was assigned to the Eighth Infantry Division Airborne School in Wiesbaden. The first thing they did was to remove all the rank from our uniforms with a razor blade; in airborne school, everyone was equally badly treated. Then they told the enlisted men they had to finish a mile run in less than ten minutes, and the officers had to finish in six minutes. Another challenge!

I later learned that I was the only one who had taken them seriously, and I finished in 5:40 running in combat boots. Finishing first, though, taught me a lesson about the importance of anonymity. "Oh, so you think you're fast, do you?" I had to carry the company flag on our runs. I had to run about five steps in front of the group, holding the flag up in the air, which made it kind of hard to run, but it was another challenge!

We then had to go through a physical training test. It was during this first morning of tests they started working on our minds too. The drill sergeants would stand beside you and yell at you to put you under pressure. At the slightest provocation, they would shout, "Drop and give me ten, soldier!" (that meant ten pushups). Many guys, especially the officers, had a real problem with hazing and reacted to it badly, which just made it worse for them because the drill sergeants were looking for points of weakness, and when they found it, they really went after it. For me, the airborne training was easy because I had learned the hard way to just be still and make myself invisible to survive it. All that fraternity hazing in college finally paid off!

Every morning, we would be up at dawn doing physical training, starting out with a run around the post. We had to run in formation. Running was my thing, and I loved to push the drill sergeants to run faster. We sang when we ran, following the lead of the sergeants.

C-130 going down the strip,
Airborne Daddy gonna take a little trip.
Stand up, hook up, shuffle to the door.
Step right out and count to four.
If that 'chute don't open wide,
I've got another one by my side.

After the physical training every day, we began to learn how to jump out of airplanes. The most important thing we had to learn was the PLF—parachute landing fall. So we spent a lot of each day learning how to jump off a three-foot-high bench and land and roll. We had to jump as if we were exiting the plane, then jump up in the air with our hands up, shouting "one thousand, two thousand, three thousand, four thousand—check canopy!"

It takes about four seconds for the parachute to open, so you must stay in that tucked position until the chute opens into a canopy above you Then you must check to make sure it's a perfect circle above you and there's not one cord mixed up and crossed so that it makes two or more canopies to catch the air (a Mae West, you figure it out), or even worse a streamer—no canopy but just a bunch of silk fluttering above your head. Of course, you also have a reserve parachute hanging in front of you that you can use if the main parachute fails.

After two and a half weeks of this, we were ready to go up and make our first jump. When we were all rigged up with our chutes on, we had to go to the drill instructors to have them check and double-check that we had everything on right. The harnesses came between our legs and then through some rings on our sides and then to a big ring in the middle of our chest, where four straps came together, called the D ring.

The problem for me was that the straps coming through our legs and the tight-fitted uniforms were very uncomfortable. So I unbuttoned my pants in front, but I didn't think it mattered since our reserve chute was hanging down in front anyway, so nothing could be seen, at least not until the drill instructors started inspecting us. A DI leaned one elbow on my reserve and got right up in my face and said, "Burrus, did you know that all your business is hanging out down there?" It caused a real laugh for all the other guys, and I got teased about it.

We were loaded on the big C-130 Hercules airplanes at dawn at the Wiesbaden Airfield. Each group of us in a line was called a *stick*. When we got to the drop zone, a red light would come on by the door. That was our signal to stand up, hook our cords to a line running the length of the plane and over our heads.

When the green light came on, the first guy in the stick was instructed to "stand in the door!" Then the jump master shouted, "Go," and one by one, we had to stand in the door of that plane going about 250 miles an hour, with our fingers on the outside of the plane (if our fingers were on the inside, there was a tendency to just hang on and stand there). Then when he said, "Go," we had to jump like we'd been taught and count to four and check our canopies. Those who didn't exit the plane quickly got a size-twelve jump boot from the DI in their butt.

The first time, I wasn't scared because I didn't know what to expect. When that wind grabbed me and threw me down the side of that plane at 250 miles per hour and that chute opened and jerked me to a slower floating speed, it really got my attention.

On the way down, I was struck by how quiet and beautiful it was just floating down under this white canopy at daybreak onto a farmer's field. I was so distracted by the experience and the view that I forgot everything about how to land. I hit the heels of my feet, my butt, and the back of my head on the ground, *ker thud!* I popped my D ring and got out of my chute, rolled it up, and ran back to the trucks to be taken back to the airbase.

We were required to do three jumps to get our Airborne Wings. The second time up, I remembered the first and was scared. When the red light came on and I stood up to hook my cord to the line, I started getting faint. I felt like all the blood was running out of my arm and down my body and that I would keel over at any moment. I honestly don't remember that jump because of the state I was in and how fast it went. But this time when I landed, I did it right, thank goodness, because the wind was blowing and I hit hard. During this second jump, a fellow officer going through the course broke his leg—end of jump school for him.

We had to do our last jump from helicopters because the planes were no longer available. It was more difficult because we were sitting on the edge of the helicopter floor, and the jump master just whacked us in the helmet and pushed us out. It was my last jump, and I got down and qualified for my wings. Enough is enough. I was ready to get back to my cushy office job.

I had taken my little Buick Skylark to Germany with me, and after two years, it bit the dust. I had just been promoted to captain and had some extra money, so I had another one of those light bulb moments: how many times in my life would I find myself with some extra money in a country with no speed limits and a desire to drive fast?

So I bought a 1970 Alfa Romeo GT coupé (3,750 dollars). Every weekend was a thousand-mile weekend. Several other officers, mostly helicopter pilots, had sports cars, and we would get together at happy hour on Friday nights and decide which ski resort or foreign city to visit that weekend. When the bartender yelled last call, we'd pair up with a girl and race to see who could be there first.

One such weekend, I paired up with my friend Patricia, and it was our turn to select the location for travel. We chose Amsterdam, and at last call on Friday night, we gave everyone the name of the pension in Amsterdam where we'd meet. It was just over five hundred miles, and we had to cross the border into Holland. We made it in five and a half hours, which also included a stop for gas and a border crossing! That little Alfa could really go!

My last year in Nuremburg, my friend Gary from OSU days returned from Vietnam and was assigned to Nuremburg. We got an apartment together, and I introduced him to all the folks hanging out at the officers' club. He hooked up with Phyllis and started going on our outings with us. One weekend, we rented a whole castle in Schloss Itter, Austria. There were a dozen couples, and we enjoyed a lavish weekend with lots of skiing, eating, dancing, and fun—great memories. Gary and Phyllis married when he left the military and have now been together for fifty years!

After jump school, I returned to my job in Nuremburg to complete the year before going to Vietnam the following summer. That last year was difficult for me professionally. I was bored with the job before airborne school and more so after it. Sure, I got in thirteen ski weekends that year, and it was fun personally, but I was becoming more and more convinced that the war in Vietnam was wrong and immoral. I was conflicted about participating, but I either had to go to Nam or go to jail. Clearly, the alternatives were not very good.

Funny thing was, I was drawn to the idea of going to Vietnam. In my generation, that was where the action was. It seemed to me that I would experience or be near the cutting edge of things there. Also, I felt a sense of responsibility. My dad's generation had done their duty and served, and so should I. I felt I had to go.

Between my time in Germany and Vietnam, the army sent me to a specialty school at Fort Eustis to learn about moving goods and people in and out of a war zone. During that school, three guys in ill-fitting suits asked for me. They took me to a private room and began to explain that because I had a secret clearance from Germany, I would need to sign a document, promising not to reveal any secrets to the enemy. I stopped them in midsentence and told them that first, Vietnam was a losing effort and an immoral war; second, if I was captured, I did not know any secrets the enemy would like, so I would cooperate fully; and third, I didn't want to go to Vietnam anyway! They promised a nasty letter in my 201 file and left. I had brought my little Alfa Romeo from Germany and spent three weekends tooling around the East Coast. I sold that car (best toy I ever owned) and left the East Coast for nothing but uncertainty. I said goodbye to my parents and flew to the West Coast.

My orders were to report to Fort Lewis, Washington, on July 26 for service in Vietnam. I had made lots of friends in Nuremburg and had lived there the first three years of my adult life, an important time for me. I had been dating Patricia for a year or more, and we had become close; saying goodbye was hard, but I wanted to go to Nam with nothing holding me back. I went through Frankfurt to process out of Transportation Command and tell Susan goodbye. She was seeing another guy then and didn't know what she would do next, so we said our goodbyes. I feared that was it. I would never see her again, and it made me sad.

Living those thirty months in Europe was a special, wonderful time for me. True, I was thrown in the deep end with my job in the military, but we had lots of free time and traveled around Europe extensively. In the next chapter, I'll describe one such trip to the Fiesta de San Fermin, the Running of the Bulls in Pamplona, Spain.

CHAPTER 3

Pamplona

Fiesta de San Fermin

When Susan got to Europe in 1969, we made several memorable trips together, the first being a trip to Spain to see the Running of the Bulls in Pamplona. That festival had been popularized in a book by Ernest Hemingway, and in fact, Papa Hemingway actually lived in Pamplona with other well-known artists in the '50s. In 1969, I had read some of Papa's books, but I did not know anyone who had ever been to the festival. It sounded like something I needed to do. So we took off a week, and in my little Buick Skylark, we headed for Spain.

After a two-day drive, we arrived in Pamplona. A town of five thousand now swelled to fifty thousand for the festival, the campgrounds were full, and every possible room and bed was booked and gone by the time we got there. But a little man approached us on the street and, with sign language, made us understand he had an apartment nearby where he would rent us a room. It was *real* cheap and *real* basic: it had meat curing in the room, hanging from the ceiling over the bed. The furniture was about fifty years old. But it got us off the street, so we laughed and went on.

We were walking down the street later and literally bumped into some friends from Oklahoma State, Lester and Sue Ann. Sue Ann was a sorority sister of Susan's, and Lester played basketball at OSU.

They ended up sharing our room because they hadn't found a place to stay either. (Ironically, fifty years later, we attended a memorial service for the legendary coach Hank Iba at OSU. Susan saw Lester, approached him, and asked if he remembered her. He looked confused until she mentioned the meat curing in our room in Pamplona, and his eyes lit up.)

The following morning, we all went downtown to the start of the festival, which always started the seventh hour of the seventh day of the seventh month every year. In the center of the town, there was a square in front of city hall. The square was completely full of people, as were all the five little streets leading to it, with everyone straining to see the mayor on a balcony, who lit the Roman candle, which signaled the start of the festival.

The crowd was surging back and forth as people from the side streets pushed to get into the square. It was frightening; if you fell, you would have been trampled or severely injured. I was holding on to Susan to try and keep her upright—me too. Of course, all the Spaniards there were full of cheap wine and feeling no pain, so they didn't care.

It was a wild scene, which was followed by dancing and singing in the streets, twenty-four hours a day for seven days. It was stiflingly hot, and there were so many people in the streets that it was claustrophobic. But we joined in and danced and sang and followed the musicians around the town in their parades with these huge, oversize heads and half bodies of saints and revered persons worn by participants. People on the balconies above us would bring out pitchers of water and throw them on the crowd to try and cool us off. We appreciated it!

The people who were really into it had costumes of white shirts and pants with red sashes around their waists and red bandanas around their necks. Some also had berets on their heads and most had bota bags slung over their shoulders full of cheap red Spanish wine. At one point, some Spaniards started grabbing Susan and feeling her all over, and I jumped in between them and turned my class ring around and shouted, "Matrimonio, matrimonio!"

They held up their hands and shouted, "Tambien!" (Me too!) and went right on. It was a wild scene.

The morning of the first running, Lester and I went down the hill, where the runners started. Susan and Sue Ann said they'd meet us in the arena. Along the way, we saw that big barricades were built at all the intersections to keep the bulls heading in one direction into the bullring at the top of the hill and center of the city. Of course, that also meant that the runners also had to run all the way up the hill and into the bullring to escape the bulls! The bulls were in a pen outside of town and about four hundred yards from where the runners started. When they fired a cannon, it was a signal for everyone to start running—bulls from fright at the sound of the cannon, people from fright of the bulls.

Lester had played basketball at OSU when I was there, and he knew that I had run track, so we both thought we could outrun a few Spaniards (we figured if we kept the others between us and the bulls, we'd be okay), so we jumped into the fray just before the cannon went off.

The Spaniards saw this running with the bulls as some kind of machismo thing where if you run before you see the bulls, you're without courage. The really brave (drunk) ones ran *alongside* the bulls, swatting them on the head with rolled-up newspapers. So when the cannon went off, most of the runners stood their ground waiting for the bulls.

Then a scary thing happened. When someone took off running, it frightened the person next to them, who started running. When one fell behind a little, he reached out and grabbed at the runner next to him to pull him back; no one wanted to be last. This made the runners scared, and so they broke free and ran even harder. Chaos, panic—a melee of bodies clutching and pulling at each other in fright, with good ole Lester and Ray right there in the middle of it all.

The morning of the first running of the bulls, we managed to break free and start to run, and when we looked back, we could see the bulls catching us. Steers were put in front to get the bulls to follow them instead of getting sidetracked and goring the runners. For the most part, it worked, but there were some who ran alongside the bulls and distracted them from their run. When that happened, the bulls would begin running at the people and scooping them up with their horns and tossing them in the air, if they were lucky. Unlucky ones were stuck through the leg or stomach with a big horn and tossed about on the horn until someone distracted the bull again. Every year, a few people are killed.

We managed to run ahead of the bulls, but when we got to the arena entrance, there was a crowd of people in a pile all trying to get in. We looked back and saw the bulls coming and saw the mess in front of us, and so we decided to do the smart thing and just jump over the fence in the square just before the arena. When I jumped up on the fence to get over, a man hit me in the shoulder with both hands, knocking me off the fence. He said, "You ran this far. You must finish the run!" So I took off, running as fast as I could, just in front of the steers and just managed to beat them into the arena.

When we got inside, we managed to get over the wall and find Susan and Sue Ann in the stands. We sat there for a while, and then the fun started in the arena. They brought yearling bulls into the arena one at a time with big rubber balls on the tips of their horns. Any crazy fool who wanted to could go out into the arena and *fight* the bull with a rolled-up newspaper.

Lester and I sat still as long as we could stand it, and then we had to get down there into it. We would stand in front of the bull, holding hands, and when the bull charged, at the last minute, we'd let go and separate, and the bull would run between us. Fun but a little bit dangerous. The only injury was a scraped knee acquired by Susan, who fell off an awning trying to get some good pictures.

Well, after that, the festival all seemed a little bit tame, so we said goodbye to our friends and started over the mountains and back to France. We made it to the Basque region between France and Spain the first night and stayed in a beautiful pension in a seaside town called San Sebastian. Next day, we drove through the Loire River Valley, where all the beautiful châteaus are.

Years later, after we married, I was attending the Thunderbird Graduate School, where I was required to be conversational in another language. I chose French, and during the summer of 1974, we went to live in France to be more proficient in the language. We spent ten weeks there, partially attending a language school and the rest just traveling and enjoying France.

CHAPTER 4

Vietnam

Our song at the officers' club in Phu Bai:
Oh Phu Bai, Oh Phu Bai, oh what a disgrace,
Oh Phu Bai, Oh Phu Bai, you're a hell of a place.
With captains and majors and light colonels too,
With thumbs up their assholes and nothing to do.
They stand on the active, they scream, and they shout,
About all those things they know nothing about.
This war is all bullshit, we might as well be,
Shoveling shit in the south China Sea.

By the end of July 1971, I was in Seattle, getting ready to board my plane for Vietnam. My good friend Doug, a frat brother and fellow hurdler from OSU, was there and insisted on throwing a party to send me off in style. He knew it was my birthday that week, and so his girlfriend baked me a nice big cake. What I didn't know was that she put some marijuana in the cake! So I showed up for my flight completely stoned. To make matters worse, when I checked in for the flight, I was informed that I was the senior captain on board, and I was to be "aircraft commander." I said, "Uh, okay."

So our plane took off from McChord Air Base on the twenty-sixth of July 1971. My birthday was the twenty-seventh, but because we crossed the international date line, we landed in Guam on the twenty-eighth. So I was never twenty-five! I guess that means

I was twenty-four twice! An episode of *M*A*S*H* couldn't have been more bizarre.

One more thing I should mention here: when I found out I was on orders for Vietnam and since I was by this time pretty much against the war, I decided if I had to go, I just wouldn't participate. I decided to try as much as possible to just not carry a weapon at all. Now it was a war zone and so, inherently dangerous, but as a captain in transportation with a year in grade, I knew I would not really need a gun most of the time. But it was my one small protest, and I succeeded. I never touched a gun during that whole tour.

We landed in Cam Ranh Bay, but I was immediately sent to Da Nang, still hopeful of a cushy office job; the army wouldn't send me to an expensive three-week school at the Transportation Command Center and then not assign me to a job to use it, would they? Wrong again! I checked into the replacement battalion, waiting for an assignment, and bumped into some officers who were heading the other way out of Vietnam.

They asked me if I needed a vehicle. I was confused by the question, and they explained. They had been working for a year in Phu Bai at the hospital there. A jeep had been damaged in a rocket attack and written off the books. It was repairable, so they fixed it up, had it repainted, and put some fictitious markings on it, "SES," on the left side of the bumper and "RUN" on the other. I asked them what unit that was, and they just laughed and said it was *nurses* spelled backward. I declined the offer; it would be just my luck to get caught with a written-off jeep and charged with a crime. That was my first glimpse of how things worked in Vietnam (just like the rest of the army), lots of chaos and trading of goods and services that had nothing to do with the war and everything to do with getting by, getting our share of limited resources, and beating the bureaucracy.

In the end, my cushy office job never materialized. I was sent seventy miles north of Da Nang to Phu Bai and assigned to the Thirty-Ninth Transportation Battalion as the headquarters company commander and S-1 (admin officer, which was a glorified secretary to the battalion commander and commander of a bunch of misfits who were strung out on drugs and couldn't drive). We had five truck companies and a total of about nine hundred men.

When I wasn't managing the headquarters company or jumping through hoops for the colonel, I spent my time doing what we know now as HR work: reassignments, promotions, writing up recommendations for medals and nonjudicial punishments. Arriving at my unit, I found out there were several guys in the battalion I had known in Germany, most of whom were junior to me. It was an easy transition to this job.

Just after I got there, I decided to go out on one of the convoys to see what it was like. I rode with one of the troops to get the feel of the battalion, more or less, having arrived three days prior to this, to ask some questions of the troops and see which way the wind blows. I never got the chance!

I was placed in a five-ton tractor with a heavy twenty-ton load on the back. The driver was a grizzled old spec 4. He was thirty-six years old (most guys of this rank were twenty-one) and earlier had gotten out of the army to go back home, only to reenlist and be sent back to Nam.

As I got in the truck cab, he grunted an acknowledgement of my presence and turned to the convoy commander, who had jumped up on the running board of his truck and grabbed the front of his shirt and told him to lead the convoy back to base camp. He was an excellent driver, keeping exactly the proper interval, maintaining proper speed (even without a speedometer), and being extra cautious of all the Honda motorcycles and small vehicle traffic. That's how I met *Pappy*. I learned later that he's as famous for his drive and competence as he is for his personality, and the legend grows each day he makes those unheard-of twelve- and fourteen-hour turnarounds up to the border and back through hostile territory.

By this time in Vietnam, morale had cratered, and it was hard to find anyone who believed in what we were doing over there. The senior officers and senior enlisted men would disappear into a beer bottle in the officers or noncommissioned officers' clubs, the draftees would get stoned on marijuana or worse, and the junior officers like me were left to try and keep everyone alive. When a soldier was caught doing drugs or suspected of being stoned, he couldn't drive a truck, so he would be transferred into headquarters company for me to deal with. I had to read so many soldiers their Miranda rights and proscribe nonjudicial punishment that even now, I can still remember the speech as I learned the army version word for word.

When I arrived in Vietnam, our job was to deliver supplies to all the fighting units in the north of the country. But almost immediately after I arrived, our mission changed from delivering supplies to them to going out to their bases and bringing them and all their supplies back. We were finally getting out of Vietnam, and our job was to evacuate all the bases from the North Vietnamese border to Da Nang. Of course, we still had to deliver food and supplies to them, but instead of coming back empty, we now had the job of bringing them and their equipment out too. Of course, the enemy noticed all this and stopped shooting at our convoys. Why stop us from leaving?

Because my job had two parts, commander and admin officer, I ended up doing the command things during the day, and after dinner and everyone else went home, I did the admin things. For example, if a commander in one of our companies wanted a soldier to get a medal, he would send me a note and ask that I process a request for a medal. But because there were only so many medals of that type given, it depended on how well you could write up the request and how good you could make the soldier look to the review board as to who got the medals. It became kind of a game, and my writing skills were pretty good, so almost all my recommendations came back approved. It backfired because when the company commanders learned that I could work the system, they began putting more and more people in for medals, which increased my workload dramatically.

I had a recurring dream that someone would sneak into my hooch and at the last minute before my death, I would see a little man in black pajamas with a long knife slitting my throat. I had that dream weekly and sometimes more often; it continued well into my civilian life, and even now, I am an extremely light sleeper. Here's why: as I was company commander and, therefore, in charge of security of our post, I also had responsibility for manning and securing the bunker line. Our base, like all the others, had a berm, a kind of dike all the way around with little cave-like areas built into it. In front of the bunker, there were openings so the soldiers could have a full view of everything in front of their area. In front of that, there was concertina wire in several rows, and in front of that, there were trip wired explosives. So it would appear to be safe. Not so fast. I knew that the VC (Vietcong) were masters at concealment and that there had been many occasions where a VC would slither up to the wire, avoid the explosives, slither under the wire, get inside a post, and cause havoc—or worse, completely undetected.

I also knew that most of the soldiers were stoned whenever they could be, so in my mind, I knew that security was doubtful at best. So I would awaken at the slightest sound. If the generator hiccupped,

I would be wide awake. We all knew that Charlie owned the night-time, and our security was greatly tied to having light.

Occasionally, we would have a rocket or mortar attack on our base. The Vietcong would sneak up just outside the lights on the bunker line and lob mortars into our area, trying to knock out the motor pool or the workshop. Fortunately, they were bad shots and routinely shot over the whole area and into a Vietnamese graveyard on the other side.

After each one of these, the colonel would get excited and tell me to form a squad and "go out and get those guys." As gently as possible, we had to convince him that these guys were bad shots; if we got rid of them, the VC might find someone who could actually shoot straight, and they might miss the graveyard and hit the motor pool! It became a running joke, with only the colonel remaining clueless but insistent that we "go out and get those guys."

Funny as that was, our colonel was a lifer, only interested in getting his ticket punched for "command experience in a war zone" so he could get promoted to full colonel. He didn't care about us or any of the troops and routinely made decisions that put our people in harm's way. I was so worried about this that I began to keep a journal of all his bad decisions because I feared being called into court one day to testify when he got someone killed. Didn't happen, but I continued to worry for my whole time there.

One morning when I arrived at my desk in the headquarters building, a young troop came running in and said, "Captain Burrus, you better get out here quick!"

I chased him across the parade ground to a hooch with several guys standing outside. I asked what was going on, and one of them said, "He's in there." I went in alone and found Staff Sergeant Cox sitting upright in a chair, dead.

He had been injured during a prior tour and was in constant pain; heroin eased the pain, but he had gotten strung out and soon found himself hopelessly addicted. With nowhere to go for help and no one to listen, he first went to see a shrink at the hospital, who just gave him a bottle of Darvon and told him to relax, then he went to the PX and bought a fifth of Jim Beam, came back to his hooch, and in despair, drank the whole bottle accompanied by the bottle of Darvon pills. When I saw him, he was clearly gone, but I hoped we might revive him.

I scooped him up in my arms and ran for a jeep. We raced out of the post and up to the hospital, hoping someone could revive him, but he was gone. I was devastated; he worked directly for me, and I didn't see what was going on until too late.

When we arrived back at our post, the first sergeant told me the colonel wanted to see me urgently. When I entered his office, still very emotional, the colonel was angry and didn't want to hear any reason or excuse for why I'd run him off the road. I wanted to throttle the insensitive bastard, but he was the commander, and all I could do was stand there, and then I started to cry. I was really affected by Sergeant Cox's death. That made him angrier, and he dismissed me to get out; I was not behaving as an officer in this man's army. *Hate* is an ugly word, but that's the emotion I felt for him.

I was never really in combat. I was only shot at once that I know of, and that was because I was driving a jeep down a highway trying to catch up with a convoy that had departed before me, and some snipers were shooting at me. (I knew because I could hear the snap of the bullets as they broke the sound barrier over my head!)

My time in Vietnam was filled with trying to take care of my people and get my job done. For every soldier who engaged the enemy, there were approximately twenty in the rear area who supported him. The nickname given us by the frontline soldiers was REMFs (rear echelon m—— f——ers). They had a right to be cynical; we were busy trying to beat the system for our own units while they were out there fighting the war and surviving on what was left over for them when they returned from the field.

Because my job involved personnel assignments, I had a lot of flexibility to go to Da Nang and even Saigon occasionally for my job. The formal way to do that was to fill out a bunch of forms, get them signed by a bunch of officers, get some travel orders cut, take them to the airfield, and wait to be assigned a place on an airplane based on priority. The other way was to just go out to the airfield and stand by the helicopter refueling point. I'd stand there and ask the pilots where they were going and if they had any room, a sort of sophisticated form of hitchhiking. It worked well and cut the time to get places substantially. Many of the pilots were in their early twenties, some younger. They were flying multi-million-dollar airplanes and reading comic books in their downtime.

We flew high enough that ground fire couldn't knock us out of the air but not so high that we couldn't get a good look at the countryside. I was immediately struck by the beauty of South Vietnam. It really is a beautiful little country. I vowed that when this was all over some day, I'd like to come back as a tourist and really see the country. And I did, in 2015 on an Overseas Adventure Tour—loved it.

Not carrying a weapon backfired on me once when I was on a convoy, and we entered a new post. The military police, who had been struggling to keep soldiers from shooting each other, confiscated all the weapons in the convoy, and of course, they came up one short. I had to finally admit that I just didn't have one, which they thought ridiculously impossible. It worked out in the end, but I had some 'splainin' to do to an MP colonel. They thought I was nuts.

One week, for reasons never revealed, all we had in our mess hall was cottage cheese and stewed tomatoes. That's all for about three days; no steaks, no pork chops, no potatoes—nothing but cottage cheese and stewed tomatoes. Many guys just ate what was in front of them and toughed it out; others whined incessantly about the graft in the army that caused them to have to suffer so.

I was headquarters company commander, so I needed to set an example. I decided that week to change the way I looked at it. I decided that cottage cheese and stewed tomatoes would be my favorite food. I decided that I couldn't wait to get to the mess hall and have that delicacy, a little boat of cottage cheese, stewed tomatoes in the middle, a little Tabasco sauce on top—a delicacy! When others complained about it, I ate theirs too. It changed everything for me (and some of them), and even now, when I see cottage cheese and stewed tomatoes served together, I make a special point of getting it on my plate and celebrating that small victory so many years ago when I was a twenty-five-year-old US Army captain.

In February 1972, the withdrawal from Vietnam accelerated (it was a presidential election year after all, and Tricky Dick Nixon wanted to show the American people he was fulfilling a campaign promise from 1968 to get us out of Vietnam), and our unit was selected for standing down. What this meant was that all the people had to be reassigned and all the equipment turned in. The colonel and all the majors above me quickly found new jobs and left the unit. I was responsible for reassigning nine hundred guys and dealing with all the property in the headquarters company. I had some good sergeants in both areas, and we got it done very quickly.

When we went to turn our equipment in, the supply guys refused to take it. It seems that everything had to be in like—new condition so they could just issue it to the next unit. Problem was that our unit had been in Vietnam for several years, and not only was the equipment all beat up, but many of the serial numbers didn't even match what was in our books.

This seemed like a big problem to me, but my supply sergeant told me he'd handle it. Just go to the officer's club for lunch, and when I got back, he'd have it all taken care of. Sure enough, when I returned, it was all turned in with receipts to prove it—to the dump, not to the supply office. He had taken hammers to all the equipment, rendered it "unserviceable," and scrapped it all. So went the military in Vietnam.

Back to reassignments, I quickly got everyone reassigned or sent home, and I realized that everyone senior to me had already found new jobs, so I was, in effect, the battalion commander. I had some leave coming, so I filled out a request for leave and signed it both as the requester and the HQ commander, then I signed it on behalf of the colonel. I took it to Officer Assignments in Da Nang and convinced a clerk to cut the orders for me to take a one-week leave. I had gotten a couple of my junior officers cushy jobs as liaison officers at Da Nang Airfield, and when I got my orders, I went out there and told them to get me on the next plane going *anywhere*.

I caught the next flight out of Da Nang, which was going to Tokyo. The Winter Olympics were starting in Sapporo, and I thought I could go up and see it. Of course, all the tickets were long since sold out, so that plan failed. I called Susan, who was by this time teaching elementary school at Clark Airbase in the Philippines. I caught a commercial flight from Tokyo to Manila, where she picked me up, and we had a grand time exploring that part of Luzon for a week. (By the way, when I went on R & R at Christmas time, it was to Taiwan, and when I walked off that plane, Susan had flown there to meet me, and I was the envy of everyone on the plane: the only guy with an American girl waiting for him on R & R.)

Toward the end of the week, I called back to Officer Assignments in Da Nang, and they said that they'd been looking for me, and I thought, *Oh, no, now I'm in trouble!*

They explained that a new rule had come down from the Pentagon: anyone with less than five months left to serve could go home and get out. I was not scheduled for reassignment but was going home and getting out. I said, "I'll be right there!" I caught a hop from Clark Airbase to Saigon and then hitched a ride back to Da Nang. I went to Finance and picked up my records, ready to go home.

I realized that it was the end of February, and if I waited three days until the first of March, I could get another month of combat pay, so I hung around the officers' area until March 1. In a few short days, in early March 1972, I found myself back in Seattle and out of the army for good. I had tried lamely to get a job with one of the sea container companies with offices in Saigon, but there was such a problem with drugs at all levels that the army told me no one could get out of the army in Vietnam. We all had to go back to Fort Lewis and pee in the bottle to prove we were clean.

I went to Vietnam as a patriot not believing in the war but believing I was doing the right thing by serving my country. I also held out some hope that we were helping a small country defend itself against communist aggressors. I learned while I was there that the Vietnamese hated us only because our presence there brought the bombs and guns, which they inevitably got in the way of. They were simple rice farmers and peasants; they didn't care about politics or communism or any of that stuff. They just wanted us to go away and stop the war. Ho Chi Minh had fought for the Americans in WWII on the condition we'd give him his country back when it was all over. We betrayed him and let the French have their colonies back. So he had to go to Russia and China to get guns to kick them out of his country. Communism was a side issue. It was a rude awakening. I came home a very cynical young man; unfortunately now, a cynical old man.

In theory, I had a six-year commitment to fulfill, and I was offered the job of Oakland Army Terminal officer as a reservist. But by this time, I was so fed up with the army that I just never responded, and in less than three months, I was back in Europe, vagabonding around.

CHAPTER 5

Okay, Tell Me a Joke

Early on in my travels, I'd been hitchhiking for a while and found myself at the border of Austria and Germany. I waited and waited, and about four hours later, as storm clouds gathered overhead and I had seen what seemed like thousands of cars race by, I got desperate. I tore the back off my notebook and wrote, "I TELL JOKES," in big letters. Soon, a big BMW skidded to a stop, and a lady rolled down her window an inch and said, "Okay, tell me one."

I said, "Did you hear about the man who went to a psychiatrist and said he thought he was a dog? 'I bark all the time, eat dog food, and crawl around on all fours.'

"The doctor said, 'Why don't you climb up here on the couch, and we can talk about it?"

"The man replied, 'Oh, I'm not allowed on the couch!'"

She laughed and told me to hop in. That's how I met Mrs. Schaditz and her son Max. We spent the next couple of hours getting to know each other. She took me to her home in Munich, fed me, and sent me downtown with her kids to experience the Hofbräuhaus. She gave me a nice bed for the night, a wonderful breakfast of "Spiegel eier mit schenken," and then dropped me off at the train station. Lesson learned: when you really need a ride, you can't show it. People don't want to pick up someone who looks distressed; they don't want any part of your problems. If they are going to pick you up, it will be because they want some company or because you look interesting. It's just human nature.

I got out of the army on March 3, 1972, in Seattle. I had no job or prospect of one, no wife or prospect of one, and ten thousand dollars I'd saved in Vietnam. Free now after four years in the military, I could do whatever my heart desired. But what was that? I said to myself, "You have seen a glimpse of the world in the army. If you don't go and see more of it right now, you'll hate yourself when you're fifty!"

I spent some time preparing, arranged for a student trip to Russia later that summer, investigated the cheapest way for a one-way trip to Europe, and bought a car, a 1972 Volkswagen Beetle convertible, orange-red with black top, 2,750 dollars! When they told me the price, I pulled out my checkbook to pay for the car. The salesman said, "Do you expect me to take a check on an Oklahoma bank and let you drive out of here with my car?" So naive was I that I just assumed he'd take it.

My dad stepped between us and said, "He just got back from Vietnam, doing his job. Now you do yours. Take his check. I'll stand behind it." Never so proud to be old Sandstorm's son. I immediately drove that little Beetle to Colorado and tried to salvage a lost ski season.

The last day of the trip, I drove from Indianapolis all the way across Kansas and Eastern Colorado in one day (1,087 miles). I arrived at my friend Doug's house late and frazzled. His girlfriend told me I needed to chill, and we smoked some marijuana. That did the trick! (The year before, they had come to Seattle to see me off for Vietnam and baked a cake with a couple of ounces of marijuana in it, but that's another story!)

I also connected with some old girlfriends in Colorado. I managed to salvage some other stuff I'd missed out on in Vietnam. Finally, in May of 1972, I left the Beetle with my folks in DC, jumped on an airplane, and flew to Frankfurt. From there, I traveled in twenty-seven countries in Europe and thirteen countries in Africa over the next sixteen months.

The trip started in Nuremburg, where I'd been stationed for thirty months. Almost immediately, I started feeling sick, so I went to the army hospital and was diagnosed with hepatitis A. I think I had contracted it eating a dirty popsicle while on a convoy in Vietnam. That delayed the start of the trip while I convalesced.

When I felt well enough, I hitchhiked down to Italy, where my cousin Glen was serving as fuels management officer on an air force base. I spent a few weeks recovering with him and his family and then hitchhiked back to Nuremburg. And that's when I met Mrs. Schaditz and had that great experience hitchhiking.

So far, the hitching was fun but very inefficient. Back in Nuremburg, I decided to buy a Volkswagen bus in which I could both travel and sleep. Hitchhiking was interesting, but traveling in my own bus was more flexible and fun. I had better control of my time, and I could avoid the cost of paying for lodging. I found one for sale by a GI and bought it for 350 dollars. I drove that van twenty thousand kilometers through Europe and finally sold it in Madrid eight months later (minus fourth gear) for three hundred dollars.

After a day of hassles and bureaucracy, I finally got the van bought and registered, and I took off from Nuremberg for the next leg of my big adventure. Initially, I drove through Luxembourg, picking up a hitchhiker along the way. I drove through Eastern France and after picking up another person, a girl from New York, we drove on to Paris. The girl and I hit it off; she was a child of the '70s like me, and a little romance ensued that night. We camped in the Bois de Boulogne. Then I did a dumb thing: I left on an airplane and gave the keys to the van to the hitchhiker, telling him I'd meet him in two weeks. Now it seems like a stupid thing to do, but at the time, I was not into owning stuff, and it just didn't seem like a big deal.

The flight to Russia had to go through Stockholm, where all the people on the tour met and then travel together to Moscow. In 1972, Russia was a very closed place, the cold war was in full steam, and after sixty years of communism, the place was falling apart in every imaginable way. Before we started the tour, the guide, supplied by the Russian tourist office, insisted that we elect a "tour leader" who could advise the guide on where we wanted to go, when, etc. After we elected our leader and discussed where we wanted to go and what we wanted to see, the guide presented our leader with a preprinted itinerary with dates and times already fixed for the next two weeks. Ha!

My first impression of Russia was that it looked bleak and drab. I noticed there was a lack of service; no one seemed to care to give us service at all. My take on this: without the free enterprise system, there's no incentive to serve, no profit for the individual. There were lines of people outside every store. Walking into the stores, we saw the shelves were bare.

One thing really impressed me in Russia: the cultural heritage. We saw art museums that opened our eyes to a history about which we were basically unaware. Of course, the ballet was incredible. I had never been to a ballet, and to see my first one in the theater where it is seen to be the very best was a treat.

Our first tour was to the "Exhibition of Economic Achievement of the USSR," a huge fairgrounds-type place with propaganda exhibits extolling the virtues of the communist system and the successes of it all. This was a precursor of things to come. For the next two weeks, all we got was propaganda about the virtues of the socialist system versus ours. Now, we could see that things were falling apart all around us, so it was an interesting contrast; if you say things are good and in the absence of anything to the contrary, they must be good.

Things didn't improve as we traveled from Moscow to Kiev and then on to Leningrad (now Saint Petersburg). Every day, there was at least one and sometimes two tours of museums dedicated to Lenin. On giant billboards, we saw slogans like, "The will of the people to have peace will not be denied!" or "Peace, Friendship, and Cooperation for the People of the World" or "End the Vietnam War." I took some heat for that last one because all the others on the tour were idealistic students and castigated me for participating in such an immoral war.

Border crossing, Europe

In Kiev, we met some guys who wanted to trade with us. They were walking behind us, saying, "Adidas, Jockey, Levis," to get our attention. Those were the only words they knew in English, so we took them up to our rooms, and they bought our underwear, and someone sold them some jeans in return for things like solid brass Russian Army belt buckles. Of course, this trading was illegal, and we thought we were being followed by the KGB, so we were paranoid the rest of the trip.

While in Leningrad, it was unusually hot that summer, so we had our shorts on. Well, the Russians never wear shorts, and we had catcalls, asking if the dogs had chewed the bottom of our pants. Once, we were sitting in a big rose garden, when a very drunk Russian staggered up and started harassing one of the kids on the tour. He was a Jewish kid, Howie, from New York. I said something that made the others laugh, and this obnoxious Russian flipped his cigarette ashes in my lap. At that point, I had enough of him, so I stood up and got in front of the goon and asked him why he didn't pick on someone his own size. It was a tense moment, but he eventually staggered off.

I was later told by the guide that I was very lucky because if it would have come to blows, it would have been very bad for me and for her.

There was a girl on the trip from Oregon named Gail, and she and I hooked up on the trip, slept together when we could get away with it, and had some fun. By the time we got to Leningrad, we were both totally fed up with all the Lenin bullshit, so we faked stomach aches and ditched one of the tours. When the bus left, we took a blanket from the hotel and went down to the river across from the Palace of Peter and Paul.

We were followed by some guys carrying a gym bag and looking very suspicious. At the beach, they sat down about five yards from us and fiddled with something in the bag. I was getting a little worried about this when I heard a click, and music started coming from the bag. He smiled big and said, "Creedence Clearwater Revival!" He had been taping music off a free station in Helsinki. We spent the day with them, new friends. Once again, I learned that friendship knows no nationality or boundary.

The most interesting things for me in all of Russia were in Leningrad: the Palace of Peterhof and the Hermitage Art Museum, both spectacular and unique. The trip ended on July 12 in London. I thought to myself, *This will be the last group trip like that for me, ever. I'm not a group trip kind of guy.*

At the end of the trip, Gail and I stayed together for a few days. We stayed at a youth camp outside of London in East Acton. It had big army tents set up—one for men, one for women, and one for couples. Of course, it was the '70s, and they were all mixed up with couples in all of them. But it cost only thirty-five pence—at the time, about a dollar—per night. After a few days enjoying each other, I said goodbye to Gail and decided to get on with my trip and retrieve my van.

Before I left London, I connected with a cousin of my father, whose husband was involved in drilling for oil in the middle east. The seven-day war was going on in Israel, and so I asked my host how a small country like Israel could possibly fight and win against all the well-funded and supplied Arab countries. He told me that he had never met any two Arabs who could agree on anything! So how could they work together to defeat the Israelis?

I left London on the twenty-third of July. I hitched a ride most of the way, and at the back of a long line of cars, I got out and walked several miles to the ferry for the passage to Ostend, Belgium. It was the start of the school holidays in England, and so it seemed everyone wanted to go to France for holidays.

In Belgium, I got off the ferry and tried to get a train to the little town in which we had agreed to rendezvous. After a little work trying to convince the station master that there really was a town called Neufvilles, Belgium, I was able to buy a ticket. I don't remember why we chose that town in which to rendezvous or how many miles he'd put on the van or very much at all about that guy. It speaks to my frame of mind at the time. I found the van in good condition and headed back to Nuremburg, which had become my home base.

I met a girl from Las Vegas at the officers' club who was visiting a teacher family. We hit it off, and she was interested in seeing more of Europe but afraid to go by herself. I offered to do the driving, she the cooking, and we'd split the gas money. Her name was Cindy, and she was an artist. The Volkswagen van was blue, and in honor of my Blue Goose panel truck back in my college days, we named it the Blue Goose II, which she painted on the side of the van. We outfitted the van with provisions from the store in Nuremberg and set off for Yugoslavia and points south.

Just traveling through Europe

My plan was to travel through the Balkan states, Greece, and Turkey, and return to Munich in time for the 1972 Summer Olympics starting in August. I thought I might have some friends competing, and I knew that Hank Iba, the legendary basketball coach from OSU and friend of my father, would be coaching the US basketball team. I had hoped some of those connections would get me into the games in some support role. In the end, it was not to be.

By this time on my trip, I learned some stuff about vagabonding.

- There's an inverse relationship between time and money with respect to travel. If you must be in Paris for breakfast tomorrow, you can do it, but it will cost you plenty. But if you have infinite time to get to Paris, you can do it for almost nothing.
- Never get in a hurry when you don't have control of the transportation. When you are depending on others, whether hitchhiking or just traveling on an airplane, it's best to just relax and let it happen. This is also true as a basic rule of vagabonding: most people are in a hurry. If you run into trouble somewhere, just wait them out.
- Most people in the world are kind, generous folks if you give them a chance to be. As you travel, extend the hand of friendship and kindness with a smile, and a world of loving kindness will come to you.
- The contrary is also true: if you travel with a smirk of fear on your face, clutching your belongings as if the next person you see will try to steal them, staying only in *safe* places and fearing everything and everyone, that's what you'll get—suspicion, fear, and maybe the one-in-a-hundred guy who wants to do you harm will do just that.
- People everywhere are concerned about some basic things every day: where and what will they eat, where will they put their head down tonight, and where can they look for some joy today? If you just understand that you have a lot more in common with them than difference and empathize with their plight, you will connect easily and find instant friends everywhere you go.

Camping sauvage

In France, they have a name for the way we traveled and camped: "camping sauvage"—literally, savage camping, which means we did not stay in regular campgrounds. We tried to just pull off the road and find some creative camping place in a forest or on a hill or by a beach or even in an abandoned field. We were self-contained in the van, so we didn't have to really "make camp," and we could stop anywhere.

We stayed off the autobahns because the van could not go as fast as they did and because we wanted to really go slow and see the places we were passing by. We drove through some old cities: Regensburg, Rosenheim, Chiemsee, and then through a tunnel into Italy. We stopped at my cousin Glen's home in Northern Italy again for a day, and then on July 30, we took off for Yugoslavia.

At that time, all the smaller countries which then made-up Yugoslavia did not exist, and it was all just the one communist country controlled by the USSR. It was possible to drive through there but not yet common to do it, so we were a little apprehensive about visas, travel restrictions, etc. Our concerns were unfounded because we quickly got visas at the border and headed south along the Adriatic Coast.

I was expecting the drab backwardness of Russia but was pleasantly surprised to find Yugoslavia a very beautiful country, more like Monaco with the mountains coming down to the sea. We drove south on the Adriatic coast road through Opatija, Zadar, and Rijeka, picking up some hitchers along the way. They helped with the gas (a condition I always put on anyone catching a ride with us), food, and water and left us with a nice little gift for giving them a ride. We arrived in Dubrovnik during the summer festival and were entertained by the festive and musical atmosphere. We left the hitchers there and continued down the coast.

Picking up three more hitchers, all French girls, we drove on through Titograd to Skopje. It was a mountain road with lots of changes in altitude. With the rain and crazy drivers, we saw more than ten big wrecks, so it was not a fun day.

Another thing that added to the stress was the gypsies, lots of them begging along the road. Some of the kids would jump on the side of the van, asking for money when we slowed down. So that day at least, we did not free camp for fear of the gypsies harassing or worse. Another problem was the donkey carts on the road. I decided not to drive at night anymore when I came up on a farmer on a donkey cart, no lights, and almost ran over him. In Skopje, we finally broke down and bought some cooked food and found the meat on a stick very good.

By this time, we had traveled over 2,500 kilometers in the Blue Goose II. It had drunk only one quart of oil, and for a ten-year-old van, I thought that was pretty good.

At the Greek border, the guard was unhappy about my appearance since by that point, I didn't look much like my passport. I had grown a beard and longer hair and didn't look at all like Captain Burrus anymore. The guard was demanding that I shave the beard before he could confirm that I was in fact the guy in that picture. At that point, I learned another rule of the road: if you just slow down and wait long enough, in most cases things, will work out. When the guard realized that I was prepared to wait until he changed his mind, he did.

We arrived in Athens two days later after spending a short time in Thessaloniki and picking up more hitchers, from England this time. After three hard days traveling, we took some time to check into a proper campground and get some hot showers and rest.

Athens was amazing. The Greek culture is different from other places, and the Greek people are genuinely friendly and helpful to anyone. We were wary after the gypsy encounter in Yugoslavia but quickly learned that what you see is what you get in Greece, and you usually get it with a big smile. Here's what I wrote in my journal of August 6, 1972:

> As we walked around the streets of Athens, we stopped at a souvlaki stand to eat. I gorged myself on them since they tasted so good and made smiling faces at the Greeks walking by. Everyone returned our smiles and wanted to engage us. That's the first time anything like that has happened in five months of traveling around and put the Greeks on the top of the list in smiles.

When we ask directions, they don't tell us the way; they *take us there* arm in arm. Great people.

We hit all the tourist spots and really enjoyed the sound and light show at the Acropolis. It was done by the people of France, who had originated the sound and light show concept, where they tell the historical story of the place with narrative, music, and changing lights on the antiquities. We also hit the flea market and were pleasantly surprised at the prices—very reasonable.

After parking the van and putting a tarp over it, we took an overnight ferry to Chania on the island of Crete, sleeping on the deck to save money. In Chania, we camped on the beach and had the police come and say, "Sleeping on the beach is forbidden but okay," typical of the easygoing attitude of all the Greeks. After checking our bags in Chania, we took a bus to the top of the Samaria Gorge, the deepest in Europe, which reminded me of a small Grand Canyon, but so narrow at the bottom, you barely see the sky. We hooked up with a couple of guys from California and decided to hike down the gorge. It took us about eight hours to hike down, and after a boat ride and bus ride, we didn't get back to Chania until late.

We drove the next day to Heraklion in a rental car shared with the guys from California. We spent the day there before returning to Athens on the ferry. In Heraklion, we visited the site of the palace of Knossos, four thousand years old. It was very interesting but mind-blowing to think that this place predated most of what I have ever studied in history or church.

In Athens, as we should have expected, the tarp was like a beacon, saying, "Break in and steal some stuff," so when we got there, we found the van had been ransacked. There really wasn't much to steal so not a big problem, but we still felt violated.

We went to the Lotus Travel Bureau, where for a few drachmas, I was able to purchase a fake student ID, and since they reduced my age from twenty-six to twenty-four, I was eligible for student things not available before. Then we took off for a tour of the Peloponnesian Peninsula. For the next few days, we established a routine that was brilliant: we drove the roads of the peninsula and stopped when we saw something interesting. At 4:00 p.m. every day, we took the next road toward the sea. It proved a good plan since we found several small fishing villages with little uninhabited beaches and friendly people. At one, Porto Genero, it was kind of a horseshoe bay with a stream feeding it, and water in the bay was part salty, part fresh. We could swim and dive with our eyes open. The beach was small white stones—perfect.

Peloponnese was the site where the ancient Greek culture was best preserved, so there were lots of ruins and amphitheaters of antiquity to see and experience. The UCLA guys were still traveling with us, so we had a lot of fun exploring the antiquities. Finally, after traveling with those guys for a week, we took them to the airport at Corinth and said goodbye.

Greece was fun, but it was time to move on. We stopped in Thessaloniki and Alexandropolis just long enough to see a little and move on again. In Greece, we saw some funny road signs that had been translated to English rather awkwardly:

ATTENTION: WAY OUT WORKSHOP

Translation: the way out of the mountains has work being done on the roads.

Dangerous Rolls and Curves

Translation: there will be dangerous curves on the mountain roads.

We also met some interesting people in Greece: one man who, with his two sons, stopped to help push us out of the sand when we were stuck on the beach; another man who was tending his sheep and told us of his simple existence with his German wife. Many Greeks and Turks went to Germany in those days as *gast-arbeiters* (guest workers) to do the manual labor and make more money than they would have in their country. Some also married German ladies and brought them back to their homeland.

After we crossed the border on the way to Istanbul, a big truck threw a rock up and hit my windshield, shattering it into pieces. It's at times like these that you really get to know a place and understand it from the ground up. We limped slowly into Istanbul to find a windshield for a ten-year-old Volkswagen van. At that time, there were hundreds of old American and European cars running around Istanbul, most were 1950s vintage. Where they came from and how they got to Turkey, I haven't a clue because nowhere else in Europe did you find American cars at all, either old or new, unless it was near a military base. On the divided highways and streets of Istanbul, there were cars going both ways on both sides of the road, and most of the stoplights had bullet holes through them. So driving there wasn't chaos, but it was close to chaos and much worse than anything we had seen in Greece.

We stopped and asked how we could get our windshield replaced, and after many stops and much hand-waving and pointing, we ended up in a small street in the bowels of old Istanbul, where auto window replacements are done. Somehow, someone managed to come up with a replacement for my 1962 Volkswagen van, and in a short afternoon, we got our windshield fixed and a door lock repaired for twenty dollars and a nice lesson in how things get done in Turkey. Backward as it was at that time, we got it fixed probably as fast as we would have (maybe faster) than if we were anywhere else in Europe or even the US.

While we were there, Cindy began playing ball with some of the little street urchins who looked like they hadn't bathed in weeks. I did some simple Harlem Globetrotter-type stuff with the ball, and when we left, about twenty kids ran a couple of blocks, shouting, "You come back tomorrow."

We found a cheap campground ten kilometers west of Istanbul and went back and forth each day to experience this fascinating city. I had been in Istanbul with a buddy when we were both serving in the army in Germany in 1970. But Cindy had not been there, and I wanted to go again without the military haircut and baggage hanging over me.

We had a leisurely visit to the mosques and the Grand Bazaar, a huge covered market in the center of town, where you can literally get lost walking down alleys filled with goods for sale. I bought a large quantity of puzzle rings and other small things I could sell back in Germany. When traveling from Europe, Turkey is the first country with a Muslim heritage you come to, and Istanbul is the first city filled with mosques. In addition to the Blue Mosque and the Topkapi Palace, there's Saint Sophia's Cathedral built in the fourth century but now turned into a mosque.

The Bosporus, which connects the Black Sea to the Mediterranean Sea, separates Istanbul into two parts. But it does more than that: it separates Europe from Asia. On the west side, it's Europe; on the east, Asia. Anyone traveling around the world back then had to go through Istanbul and cross the Bosporus. One of the things that I really enjoyed about traveling like I did was the way you can see things you never would have even imagined at home.

At a sidewalk café, we were approached by a beggar who had a cast on his arm with a hole in the end with blood and pus dripping out of it, making it look like his hand had been amputated. If it weren't so obviously fake, it would have ruined our tea, but as it was, we were amused. Another man in the same café was walking around with a stethoscope and blood pressure cuff, offering to take peoples' blood pressure for a tip.

One more thing happened in Istanbul and nowhere else: a guy offered to change money at a very favorable rate. We went around the corner, and as he was counting out the Turkish bills, another guy came running up and shouting about the police. So the first guy tried to just return the twenty-dollar bill I gave him and run away. Before he left, I looked at the bill, and it was a one-dollar bill. I thought maybe Cindy had made a mistake because I knew she had some ones, but she said it was a twenty. I just barely grabbed the guy before he got away with my money. The lesson: don't allow greed for a good deal to cloud your judgement; if it sounds too good to be true....

Another place that was well-known back then as a crossroads between Europe and Asia was the Pudding Shop; it was around the back of the Blue Mosque in Istanbul. Hippies and vagabonds traveling from Afghanistan and Iran on their way to Europe met and exchanged travel information with people going the other direction from Europe. At the Pudding Shop, you not only learned how to travel cheaply but safely from there in both directions. We found some fellow travelers who wanted to go to Europe, and so we struck a deal to take them if they helped with the gas.

The first guy we met was Ian from Melbourne, Australia. He had traveled alone overland from Melbourne through Australia to Darwin, where he caught a boat to East Timor. Then he traveled overland through the Asian countries Afghanistan, Iran, and on to Istanbul. Quite a character. When I mentioned we needed more people to reduce the cost of gas per person, he stood up in the Pudding Shop and shouted for volunteers. Typical Aussie—fearless. Two British girls stood up, and so we now had five of us to head back toward Germany together.

What we didn't know then but later learned was that the British girls had a strange sense of personal hygiene, and after about three days, the van began to smell. Turns out, the girls had washed their clothes in Istanbul but had not had time to dry them, so they just shoved them in a couple of plastic bags and let them mildew in my van! When we arrived in Budapest, we invited them to leave.

As we drove out of Istanbul heading west, the fourth gear in the van just stopped working. It was the synchro ring that did not allow the car to stay in fourth. So we drove the rest of the way to Germany and onwards in third. That meant that we could not go faster than fifty miles per hour, which suited us just fine. Ian said, "No problem, mate! Just stick her in third, and she'll be right." Looking back, I probably should have had the transmission worked on in Turkey, where it was so cheap, and it seemed they could fix anything. But we'd already left Istanbul, so we just drove slowly.

When we arrived at the border of Bulgaria from Turkey and had already crossed the Turkish border, there was a huge parking lot with about six cars waiting to cross into Bulgaria. We joined the cue, and since no one was moving, Ian got out with the Frisbee, and we started throwing it around. Immediately, a guard came over with a loaded weapon and told us with gesture to get back in the van. Ian mouthed off to him, and even though he had no idea what was said, I could see we had trouble ahead.

When we finally got to the border station, there was a very severe-looking lady in charge, who had been informed by the guard that we were troublemakers. She basically told us that, and she didn't want our kind in Bulgaria corrupting their youth. Go away! It took a lot of talking and cajoling to get her to even consider letting us in, and then she decided she was going to inspect the van. We had to take everything out of the van, and I began to worry about my trade goods (the puzzle rings and other things) getting confiscated. I had stashed them in a cabinet in the van that was locked by a combination lock. She had never seen a combination lock before and was fascinated by it. I showed her how to open and close the lock using the combination and then she tried it. I knew then that we were going to get into Bulgaria. She took the lock, disregarded the contents of the cabinet, and gave us forty-eight-hour visas to get across Bulgaria to Romania.

By the time we got through the border, it was getting late, so we drove along and found an apple orchard with ripe green apples—just the ticket. So we drove into the orchard and hid the van. We camped there and gorged ourselves on the peoples' apples. We also found a lake and went swimming with some of the most rotund Soviet ladies we'd ever seen in small bikinis.

Crossing into Romania was a change again: very friendly people in contrast to the stiff, unfriendly Bulgarians, but it's the poorest country in Europe, and at the time, most of the people were still getting around in horse-drawn carts, no cars.

We stopped in Romania for just one night, but there was nothing to buy in the stores, all empty, and the restaurants were pretty bleak. It was really depressing, so we passed straight through Romania and crossed into Hungary but not before taking a slight detour of thirty kilometers off the main road to see the Manaateria Govora near the town of Baille Govora. It was built in 1492 and had been an active monastery ever since, the oldest in Europe.

When we got into Hungary, we went straight to Budapest. We realized immediately that we should have gotten longer than two-day visas because there was so much to see and do there. Budapest is separated by the Danube River into the Buda (old) and Pest (new) sides. On the Buda side, there was a beautiful castle where we were looking at the sites when an older lady approached us. She had kids in Germany she wanted to visit and was desperate for foreign exchange. There were restrictions on how much they can convert, so we traded money with her, and she took us for coffee and pastries (called Creamisch), a fantastic pastry. She was nice but a very sad lady, and we saw firsthand how the communist system was failing at the grassroots level. It was a nice contrast to the rest of the people we met in Hungary, who were mostly unfriendly and quite a difference from the nice Romanians.

Her family had been very wealthy; the state came in and took over her house and gave her two rooms to live in and moved some other poor people into the rest of the house. All personal property was confiscated by the state and supposedly divided up among the poor. Sounds good for the poor, but the fellows who were playing God in all this were corrupt too, so it just went from the rich to the nouveau riche; power changed hands, but it did little for the poor. Of course, the poor did not know how to take care of these mansions, so in a short time, it all reverted to squalor.

We soon crossed over into Austria. What a difference! After spending the last several days in communist countries, to come into Western Europe and feel the modernity—it was just great. It was made sweeter by a fest going on just three hundred meters inside

Austria, where we ate our first good food in days. Ian and I took turns dancing with Cindy to the oompah music at the fest and drank some beer.

We found a beautiful "camping sauvage" campsite on top of a hill overlooking the Danube River and spent our last night camping with Ian. He was a guitar player, and we sat around several campfires on the way, singing and sharing philosophies of life. Ian is the one who put me onto the idea of working in the grape harvest in France. We dropped Ian off at the autobahn entrance, and we drove off up the Danube toward Munich.

I had planned to go to the Olympics in Munich, but the day we arrived, the terrorists struck and held the Israeli Olympic team hostage, killing several of them. This pretty well ruined the spirit of the Olympics for me, so I just got back in the van and drove on. In Nuremberg, Cindy and I decided to split up. We had originally planned to go to Greece and Turkey, and that trip was finished. It was awkward because we had become close and good companions along the way, so there was some attachment there. But I was ready to move on, so I headed for France, thinking that was the last I'd seen of her.

CHAPTER 6

Bon! Vous-est Le Porter

Arriving at the house of the patron Xavier Ruhlmann, he asked me to follow him out back. He pointed at a forty-kilogram sack of fertilizer and told me to throw it in the *camionette* (little pickup). Luckily, my experience working at the Stillwater Feed Mill back in Oklahoma in high school taught me how to lift heavy objects, so I tossed it in the truck. He smiled and said, "Vous-est le porteur!" (You are the porteur) the guy who will carry the grapes out of the field and tip them into the big barrels on the back of the truck. Well, I was a proud boy now; I had a title! Little did I know how tough the next three weeks would be.

Grapes to be carried out of the field, Alsace region of eastern France

I left Nuremburg in September of 1972 headed west. My intentions were to go over to France and work in the grape harvest and then head down through Spain to North Africa. After two hundred kilometers or so, the engine in the van blew up. I found a mechanic who would replace it with another from a junkyard and, after two rebuilt engines, started out again.

I crossed over into France and went straight to the American Express office to get some money. By this time, I had only enough for one tank of gas or a few days' meals, not both. It was then that I got a shock: the Amex offices in France were not authorized to do banking, only travel arrangements. After getting through the money problem with some quick help from my parents back home, I headed for the Alsace, where I'd been told the grape harvest was in full swing.

At the local employment office, a very officious matron scolded me for asking for help finding a job in the grape harvest, but as I was leaving, a young lady at a desk said, "Psst." She handed me a slip of paper and winking, said, "My uncle."

I had a few days to kill before we started the work, and I knew they needed pickers too (oh, hell, I was missing Cindy too), so I asked her to come and work with me in this grape harvest. I picked her up from the train station in Strasbourg, and we spent the weekend in Zurich. I was still driving the 1962 Volkswagen Van, and the rebuilt engine seemed to be holding its own; the transmission, however, still only had three gears. On Sunday, we returned to Ammerschwihr, the small village just north of Colmar in the Alsace.

Xavier Rhulmann was a portly gentleman, almost as big around as he was tall. I asked him once what he did when he wasn't making wine, and he told me, "Schneiderin" (clothes maker). Not surprising since I doubted he could find clothes off the rack for his girth! His first language was the Alsatian dialect of German, his second was High German, and third was French.

In the evenings, the patron's wife would feed us a simple meal, and then we'd watch a little French TV before bed. One night, we were watching the electioneering on TV, and it was when Valéry Giscard d'Estaing was running for prime minister of France for the first time. I asked Xavier if he liked Valerie and would vote for him.

He fixed me with a stare and said very pointedly that his family had been making wine in this valley for a long time. In his lifetime, he had been French three times and German twice. Politicians come, and politicians go; he just made his wine!

You see, the Alsace is on the border of Germany and France, and during the first and second world wars, that part of France was taken by Germany. Xavier had been born before the first world war, and during the second, he was drafted by the Nazis. He didn't think much of fighting for the Germans, so he told them he was a musician. He played the tuba in the Nazi Army band, and I think he learned to play as he went along so he would not have to be a foot soldier. Sometimes, while we were just sitting around, he would put some German oompah music on and pretend to be playing his tuba again, puffing along with the music. It was comical, and I loved it!

He told me his family had been making wine in the Alsace for one thousand years; I asked him again because I thought I had a decimal wrong, but he repeated one thousand years. His wife was a quiet little woman who cooked and stayed in the background. When we arrived, she asked Cindy if she spoke English since she was from California. Like in America, people everywhere are ignorant of what's going on outside their place.

We communicated in pidgin German since I had spent three years there in the army. Xavier was skeptical about how long I'd be around. He had seen American TV programs and was convinced that all Americans were weak and lazy, not willing to work hard. I had a great incentive to prove him wrong. Cindy would be one of the pickers of the grapes. The pickers would tip their buckets into a barrel-staved cone-shaped container called the *bodisch*, which was about four feet high. The *bodisch* was sitting on a frame that could be mechanically cranked up to a height that allowed me to climb into rucksack-like straps and stagger out of the field with sixty to seventy pounds of grapes, climb a ladder, and tip the whole load into larger barrels on the truck.

In this area, there were many grape vineyards of fifty to one hundred acres, each of which had a different type of grapes. Xavier, the patron had a few rows of grapes in each field, and each type of grape made a certain variety of wine. We would pick in a field and then move to another field. We began each day at dawn, at least I did. The patron would wake me at daybreak in my little space in his attic and bring me downstairs for breakfast, which consisted of porridge, bread (which his wife had already been to the boulangerie and bought), and coffee. After we ate the porridge, we used the bread to clean out the bowl and the coffee poured into the same bowl.

The patron made his own schnapps, which was at least one hundred proof (fifty percent alcohol content) and would pour some into his bowl and push the bottle across the table for me to do the same. I tried to resist, but he insisted and would put about two fingers of this "lightning in a bottle" in my coffee. My head didn't usually clear until about three hours later.

Our work crew was an odd assortment of people, most of whom only spoke French. Cindy didn't understand a damned word they said, so she gave them all nicknames. First was "Cretin Maurice," who walked around all the time with a stupid grin and looked like Maurice Chevalier. Next was "Granddaddy Little Boy," a man of about seventy from Dijon, who had been coming to help with the grape harvest for twenty-five years, and his buddy "Old Smacky Lips," who did that with his lips when he ate and finished every sentence with the word *tack*, like an expletive for effect. Finally, there were two guys who outworked all the others: "Good Guy," who was from Kayserberg, and Lucien, the patron's son-in-law, who was a mechanic in a garage in Colmar most of the time but always helped with the harvest.

For most of the time, it was only Lucien and me who were *porteurs*. We had to really hustle to keep the pickers from having to wait on us with their full buckets. Some of the time, I was running back to the field from the truck. When I did this for a couple of days in a row, the patron was elated. His *porteurs* were usually Spaniards or Turks who didn't do any running and lasted until they got a week's pay and disappeared. When I worked hard and stayed, he decided I was okay and began to treat me with respect.

When it was time to sit and discuss where we would work the next day, he would ask me to come and sit by him. "Raymond, vien toi ici!" (come here, sit by me) I couldn't contribute of course because I had little idea what they were saying, but I was included. From the beginning, the older guys and even the patron would ask me, "Mooder?" (Tired, yet?), and I'd always answer, "Ein bischen" (just a little), which would crack them all up, knowing I must be completely whacked by then.

At one point about a week into the work, after we'd been working on a steep hill all day, at the end of the day after dinner, I tried as casually as possible to ask the patron if we were going back to the "hoch platz" (high place). I didn't know how to say the right words, and they all got a big laugh out of that, first because it was my first slight admission that I was feeling the work more than a little and second because I'd mangled the language.

After each day's picking, we would go back to the winery and dump all the grapes into a crushing machine that mashed all the liquid out of the grapes. The grapes that were left were put back into some barrels and left to stand for a while and then resqueezed for the patron to make his lethal brand of schnapps for his own consumption. The patron had borrowed some barrels from friends in the village, and he would have me put an empty barrel on my shoulders, and then he would strut (waddle, really) down the street with me behind him, staggering along under the weight of the barrel. When people would lean out of their windows, he would say, "Mon Americaine," as if to say, "I'm the only one in this village with an American working for them!"

People would come from all over France to go through the winery during the harvest. I would be working in the barn, cleaning up the mashed grapes, and he would walk by with his tour group and nonchalantly hook a thumb over his shoulder and again say, "Mon Americaine," very proudly. These people were the sons and grandsons of his father and grandfather's customers. He did not sell his grapes to a cooperative association and get paid for the juice based on its sugar content as many of the other vintners did. He was very proud of the fact that he sold all his wine to people who came to his winery and bought it.

One day after work, Lucien, the son-in-law, invited me to go over to his brother's place, where I thought we were going to sit around and drink wine and take it easy. Not so! I ended up working another couple of hours, getting more grapes out of the field. I overheard Lucien tell his brother, "Er hat kein angst fur arbeiten!" (He has no fear of hard work!) Felt good.

On the weekends, the students would come from the university in Strasbourg and help with the picking. There was a dozen or so more pickers and only one more *porteur*, so the work intensified for us. After work, we sat around and talked; that's when I learned there's a family in the Alsace named Burrus, who own a tobacco company. The university kids thought it funny that someone with an obviously French name, Raymond, and an Alsatian family name, Burrus, couldn't speak French. I vowed someday to return and correct the problem.

After two weeks of work, the patron came up to the attic room as I sat on the bed, packing my things to leave and said, "Can you stay and help my brother?" His brother had a heart attack the day before, and someone had to help harvesting his grapes. I had been there for three weeks already, and I was tired of working in the grape harvest. We had just finished getting all his grapes out of the fields; it was November. Over those three weeks, we got a good glimpse of life in the Alsace. It was an education we could never afford if we had to buy it. But it was time to go. I had summer clothes and needed to go south.

He offered to buy me a sweater. I tried to explain that I was doing this for the experience and really needed to go. He offered me more money, and I kept saying, "Xavier, it's not about the money, really!" I finally realized that he really needed me, and I had to stay. It took us another week to finish. I let him keep the money. Finally, it was time to go. Xavier hugged me like a son and bid me farewell as I drove away in my Volkswagen van.

That was just over forty-eight years ago. It was only three weeks but a very meaningful three weeks in my life. I learned about these people of the earth who work hard every year, and for a short time, I got to toil alongside them. I got to step inside a culture that differed from my own that had changed very little for several hundred years. And I made a friend for life in Xavier Ruhlmann.

A postscript

A couple of years later, I had finished vagabonding and spent a year in graduate school. The school required that I be conversational in another language, and I chose French. My wife Susan and I spent the summer in France, and we went to the Alsace one weekend. I found the patron's house and stuck my head in the back door and said, "Patron! C'est moi, Raymond!"

He looked at me with a puzzled expression and, in German, said, "No, it's impossible. My Raymond only spoke German."

After some convincing, he jumped up and hugged me like a long-lost son. I explained about the confusion of two languages, and we spent the afternoon reminiscing. He took me down to the winery and offered to let me take as many bottles as I could carry. That was the last time I ever saw him.

CHAPTER 7

Buenos Noches, Senor!

When Cindy and I left the Alsace, we went to Zurich. There, we had a small-world experience. We went to a small restaurant and sat next to some Americans, and they overheard our conversation. In talking to them, we learned they were from Berkley, where the guys we traveled with in Crete were from. I asked them if they had heard of a guy named Steve M. Their mouths dropped open, and one of them said he was Kelly M., Steve's brother. Now our mouths dropped open! Steve had told his brother about our trip to Crete and described us to him and now, here we were five months later, meeting his brother in an obscure coffee shop in Switzerland. We also met Magdy W., an Egyptian medical student studying in Switzerland. He regaled us with stories about Egypt.

We spent a couple more days in the mountains and then headed for Spain. We drove through southern France to Andorra in the Pyrenees Mountains. I was still driving the old Blue Goose, still with only three gears. Cindy was still painting the high points on the side of the Goose.

After we left Andorra, we drove through northern Spain and camped along the way. One night, we waited until after dark, which was too late, and found a campsite on top of a small rise away from the road. It seemed harmless enough. We made camp, had dinner, and got ready for bed. We were sitting in bed with the little reading light on when I heard a tapping at the window. When I looked out,

I was staring down the barrel of a rifle; there was a whole squad of Spanish soldiers. The one who tapped on the window said, "Buenos noches, senor." It was funny when we recalled it later, but it scared the crap out of me when it happened. We had stumbled onto a military reservation and were camping in the middle of a firing range! We got off that hill and found a safer camping spot, pronto.

We drove into Madrid, and we stayed in the Plaza Mayor area, Pension Soledad. It was cheap (1.50 dollars a night). We visited the museums and other tourist places and left the car parked on the street. When we returned, the car was gone! We went to the police to report it stolen and learned that it had been towed. Apparently, there was a law about leaving an abandoned car on the street in Madrid for more than two days. So after much communication problems, we finally found the car in an impound lot and had to pay the fine for illegal parking, the towing, and storage in the impound lot. Not fun.

I enjoyed Madrid, finding it different from other places in Europe, with its own culture and ambience, and of course, the Prado Museum was incredible. We took some side trips around Spain and Portugal, but what I remember most about that experience is how cold it gets in Spain in late November.

In Madrid, we were in Camping Osuna, and I climbed out of the van as it started to snow, complaining about the cold, and said, "We need to sell this van and go to Africa where it's warm!" The guy in the tent next to us wanted a warmer place to sleep. I sold him the van for three hundred dollars. (He didn't even know if it had an engine, much less a transmission; he just wanted a place to sleep out of the snow!)

From Madrid, with three hundred dollars in my pocket, we took the overnight train to Barcelona. We spent five days in Barcelona, staying at a place called Hostel Aragonés, very cheap. Walking around town one day and trying to decide what to do next, we bumped into an American couple who had just bought passage on a Turkish freighter for fifty dollars each, seventh class (below the waterline)! The freighter was going all the way to Alexandria, Egypt, on a five-day passage. So we went to the office where they sold tickets and bought ourselves some tickets to Alexandria, seventh class, no food.

On the first of December, we departed Barcelona on the Turkish freighter en route to Marseilles, Genoa, Naples, and then Alexandria.

As we docked in Marseilles, we got our shore passes and couldn't wait to escape to land. The passage from Barcelona to Marseilles was through part of the sea that was notoriously rough that time of the year. Some of our traveling companions were sick. We were able to find something to eat and then return to the boat in the afternoon after it had unloaded and reloaded cargo. This would be repeated each day until we left Naples for the two-day sailing to Alexandria.

We learned that the Turkish sailors understood German, so we could communicate. They threw away food from the dining room, which we did not have access to. So after every meal, we showed up in the kitchen, and the Turks gave us our choice of what they were going to toss. Our own little private buffet!

We arrived by ship into Alexandria harbor, and after the army of officials was finished with us, which included their insistence that we change hard currency into Egyptian pounds, we finally got our documents stamped and stepped onto Egyptian docks. We stepped off the boat and learned about the *kilometrage*, a pass we could buy on the Egyptian Railway that would take us three thousand kilometers, just enough to see the country. We also learned that because Egypt was at war with Israel at the time, travel any other way was severely restricted (no hitching), so we had no choice really but to take the train. Alexandria is an ancient port city, more than four thousand years old, and with lots of history and culture to explore. We walked through the Library of Alexandria, which predated the time of Christ! It was mind-boggling really for someone whose only knowledge of Egypt came from the Bible.

In Alexandria, we went to a museum at the residence of King Farouk, who was deposed in the 1950s. His opulence and over-the-top lifestyle were amazing. From the beginning in Egypt, Cindy had trouble with the men. Egypt was, at that time, a conservative Muslim place. So when a woman walks around with her arms and legs showing, it's a recipe for trouble. She had typical clothes of the time: halter tops and short shorts. Once, we were walking down the street, and some young boys were approaching. The one farthest away pushed his friend into Susan and then reached over and gave her boob a squeeze. She yelped, and they ran away.

Another time, we were on a tram; I was in front of her, and a conservative gentleman in a suit was behind her. As the tram lurched to a stop, she yelped again and turned and smacked the man behind her, who was as astonished as I was. Turns out, a boy had seen her and got on the tram behind the gentleman. As the tram stopped, he reached through the man's legs and up her skirt and gave her a little goose. She thought it was the man and smacked him.

This didn't only happen in Alexandria; it continued in Cairo, Luxor, and Upper Egypt. It caused a problem for both of us because she expected me to protect her. I think if she'd have dressed more conservatively, it would have made a big difference. As it was, she was constantly on guard, wearing a knife on her belt!

When we left Alexandria for Cairo, it was our first experience with the Egyptian Railway. Our train ride was pleasant. We traveled in luxurious comfort: air-conditioned cars, reclining seats, individually adjustable air, and lights—in fact, it was very similar to a first-class airplane ride, only you had the sensation of constantly taking off! When we rolled up the blinds on our windows, we viewed the people of the Nile River Delta. Most of them are living in mud huts, and I feel like we were finally seeing Egypt for the first time like it really is. Later, as we traveled by train into Upper Egypt, we learned that almost all the Egyptians live within a couple of miles of the Nile River; all the rest is just a big empty desert.

Arriving in Cairo, we found the same teeming mass of turban-headed Egyptians, all wearing the galabia, a long dress-like garment worn by all the men. There were also tons of beggars who constantly harass you to carry your bag, open the cab door, give you directions, act as your guide, etc. They drove us nuts, constantly yelling, "Baksheesh" (give us a tip). It's the first country of my trip where I felt this pressed by desperate people.

We found a hotel, the Claridge, for seventy Egyptian cents per night (bath, ten cents extra). This was typical of what we found all over Africa at the time. Of course, it requires you to look around for the hotels where the *people* live, not the tourists. We found something similar in Luxor, New Karnak Hotel, for eighty-two cents per night.

In Cairo, we found Magdy, the medical student we met in Switzerland at his family home. He and his sister showed us around and made a valiant effort to show us how modern and contemporary it was there, but I wasn't buying it. Like most third world countries, almost all the wealth is in the hands of a very small minority, and the rest live in poverty. We arrived back at his house one night and had to enter through the back door. The door was blocked by one of their servants sleeping on the kitchen floor. Magdy forced the door open and kicked her out of the way like a dog.

One bright spot during the visit to Egypt was discovering Pharaonic history. The Egyptian Museum in Cairo is overflowing with Pharaonic history. We saw three-thousand-year-old mummies and were told that they can only display about five percent of what they have in storage. This brief education into Egyptian history was more interesting because of the complete lack of any reference to it in a typical American education. All through Egypt, I was blown away, learning things I had no idea of and seeing it up close.

We crossed the Nile and went to Giza and saw the pyramids and rode some camels. The pyramids were marvels of architectural and civil engineering. They are actually tombs of Pharaohs, and because of the way they were constructed, it was virtually impossible to enter after the tomb was sealed. They had interlocking stones that weighed thousands of pounds, which dropped into place in geometric pattern as they departed the tomb to prevent reentry. I was impressed.

We ate in local restaurants and even on the streets from vendors. The food we liked best was called "foul and falafel" made from chick-peas and deep fried. We also liked the *tahina*, which is a sauce you dip the pita bread into. Another dish we had at a local restaurant was called *kiushiari*, which had a lot of hot chili peppers in it and, as I'll describe later, made me sick as a dog.

From Cairo, we took the train to Luxor in upper Egypt. The train tracks follow the Nile south, and the view was bleak until we came to built-up areas. Luxor was the ancient home of the kings of Egypt, and an area that is called the Valley of the Kings was just across the Nile to the west. We were offered what we thought were expensive tours to see the Valley of the Kings, but we decided to do it on our own.

We rented bicycles for part of the way and then donkeys to get to the tomb of Tutankhamun, the boy-king whose tomb was only discovered about fifty years ago. Because the kings were buried with many of their worldly possessions to get them into the next life, by discovering the tombs, the archeologists have been able to reconstruct many aspects of their life, which was very enlightening. In Luxor, there was another sound and light show, even better than the one at the pyramids in Cairo. I was continually amazed by the history of Egypt, which until that time, I was clueless about.

An interesting thing happened in Luxor. It was cold at night when we left Cairo, and not knowing what accommodations would be like later, I took a blanket out of the hotel. One afternoon, in the hotel in Luxor, there was a knock at the door, and when I opened it, I saw a little man with a long overcoat, a scarf wrapped around his head, and a heavy beard. He only said one word: "blanket." How did he know where to find me? Didn't know or care; I quickly surrendered the blanket.

From Luxor, we took the train to Aswan, which was the end of the line and where Aswan Dam backed up the Nile to form Lake Nasser. We had heard from other travelers not to miss the temple of Abu Simbel, which was on the shore of Lake Nasser a few hundred miles south of Aswan. The temple was hewn out of the side of a sandstone cliff face about three thousand years ago by the Pharaoh Ramesses II for the purpose of establishing the boundary of upper Egypt and to defend it against the Nubians from further south (now Sudanese).

We found that there was a plane that flew tourists to the temple site in the morning and back in the evenings. If we took the plane that was going to retrieve the tourists in the evening, it meant that we had to spend the night there, but hardly anyone took that flight, so we could bargain for a good fare (I think we may have been the only passengers).

As we approached the site of the temple by air, we were met with an engineering marvel. When they built the Aswan Dam, the temple was going to be flooded, so a United Nations group put together some engineering companies to try and save it. They figured out a way to literally saw it into ten-ton blocks and lift it up and back from the flooded river to the shore of the new lake. Of course, there was no cliff there, so they built up a berm of sand and earth behind it to recreate the exact look of the original temple beside the Nile. It was eventually moved sixty feet up and two hundred feet back to save it.

On the outside, the temple had two Pharaonic figures that were as tall as the cliff itself. The earlobe of one of the figures had broken off and was lying on the ground; it was as tall as me. The door to enter the temple was only as tall as the foot of one of the figures on either side.

The temple was really a three-chambered cave hewn out of the sandstone cliff. The first large room was for any Egyptian to enter and pray. The second smaller room was for the priests. And the third and last room was for the Pharaoh himself. There were three godlike figures in that room: two were gods of their worship, and the third was a figure of the Pharaoh himself because he was considered a god. The ancient engineering was so exact that only once a year, as the sun made its arc across the sky, at dawn, the sun would peak over the horizon and through the three doors and shine directly on the face of the Pharaoh! His birthday!

We arrived at the temple late in the afternoon to find a guesthouse where they charged more than we wanted to pay (about ten dollars), so we wandered around the temple and tried to find a place to sleep outside for one night. We took our bedrolls and put them down in front of the temple. It was a full moon that night, and as the night wore on, trying to sleep on the stone entryway, I was awakened several times to shift my weight or turn over. As the full moon shone on the faces of those figures guarding the temple and as the night wore on, it seemed to me that the faces were changing expression. It was eerie! One time the face looked stern; another, it looked perplexed. This continued all night long with me waking up every hour or so and being freaked out by these figures *watching* me.

Abu Simbel in upper Egypt

We returned to Aswan on the morning flight and planned to return to Cairo. Cindy was, by this time, completely fed up with the Egyptian boys pinching her boobs and bottom and wanted to go back to Germany. Also, by this time, it was approaching Christmas, and she wanted to get back for that. I was committed, however, to continue the trip into Africa. I had learned that there was a barge going up the Nile from the other side of the dam every day or so and that I could buy passage to the Sudan.

We got back to Cairo and hooked up with Magdy again; we told him we wanted to eat some *local* food. He took us to a place in the bowels of a bazaar somewhere in Cairo, and we ate something called *kiuchieri*. It tasted good, but the next day, I came down with a case of food poisoning. It was Christmas Eve. Cindy decided to stay with me until I recovered, but it was still one of the bleakest Christmas holidays ever for me. Finally, after sitting up in a chair for three days, the hotel manager sent a doctor up, and he gave me a shot in the bum and told me to go down to the Hilton and eat some bland food for a few days until I felt better.

Cindy left on a plane on December 29. I got back on the train and used up the last of my kilometrage going back to Aswan. I had an experience in a restaurant there, which was indicative of what I would see for the next seven months. I sat down and ordered some food at an outdoor restaurant, and when they brought it, there were no utensils. I asked the waiter, who had on a greasy, dirty apron, for a fork, and he reached over to another table where some people had just left, took a fork off one of their plates, wiped it on his apron, and gave it to me with a big smile. And you know what I did? I took it, wiped it on a paper napkin, and ate the food without a second thought. (Does this mean I'm a *real* traveling vagabond or just very hungry?)

Finally, it was time to begin the next phase of my adventure. I would take this barge up the Nile for several days, passing the temple of Abu Simbel by boat this time and end up in black Africa in the Sudan.

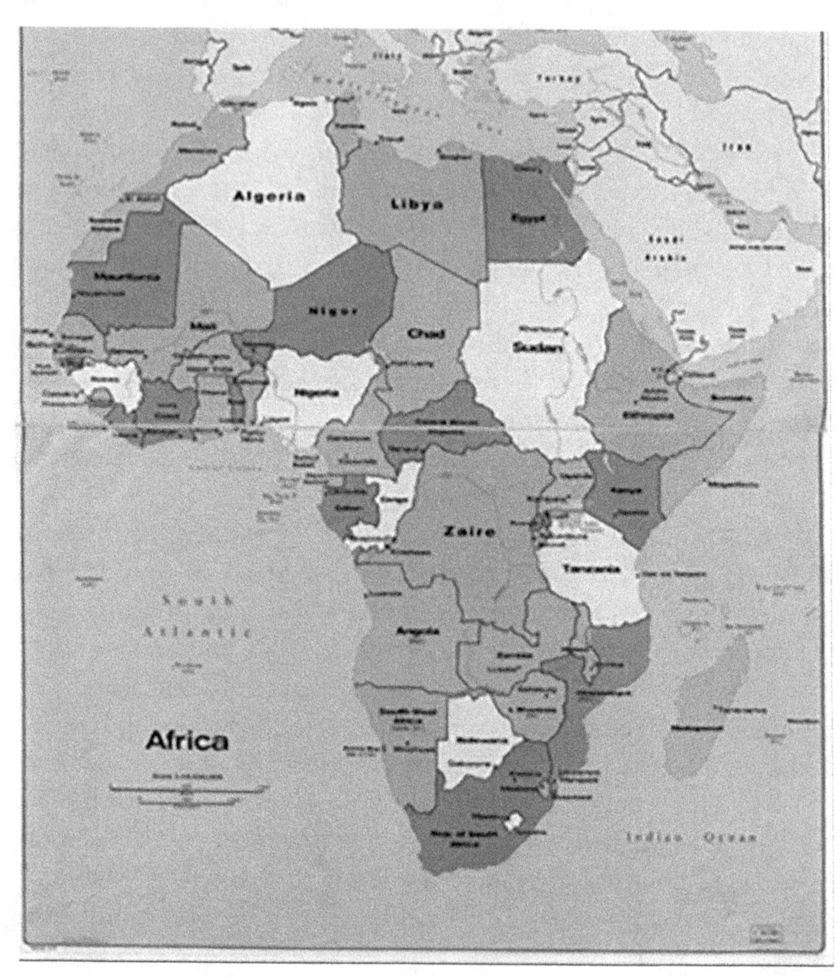

1970's Map of Africa

CHAPTER 8

Where Have All The Flowers Gone

We left Khartoum at dawn on January 11, 1973. We had been riding all day on a goat truck across the Sudanese desert. Here's my journal entry from that day:

> And finally, I felt a unique thing was happening to me. I wonder how many times in my life I'll ride across the Sudanese Desert in the middle of the night on top of the cab of a truck with a Frenchman on one side and an Arab on the other, feeling the closeness of our shared experience, singing "Where

> Have All the Flowers Gone?" And on reflection, I was much amused and thought I finally found the answer to the question which had been lurking in the back of my mind—Why? Does all this traveling around the World have any meaning? And the answer is the feeling I described above.

It was a realization that this was unique and wonderful, and I would remember it the rest of my life! And there were equally wonderful experiences to follow.

But how, you ask, did I get on a truck racing across the Sudanese desert in 1973? I had spent the month of December 1972 in Egypt. My travel companion of the previous six months was flying back to Europe. After a quick trip up the Nile, I bought a ticket from Nile Sudanese Shipping Company for 1.50 Egyptian pounds (about three dollars at the time) from Aswan to Wadi Halfa in the Sudan. Wadi Halfa is just past the border of Sudan, where a train cuts across the desert to Khartoum. I bought a few groceries and took the train from Aswan to the end of the line at the Aswan Dam, where we cleared customs and immigration from Egypt. At this point I traveled with a Brazilian, two French guys, and an Aussie.

We boarded the barge and went up to a lounge, where we dumped our bags. At our priced tickets, we did not have access to the cabins. The barge decks were covered with cargo. That evening, the cook for the deckhands on the barge served a soup of lentils and beans. We could eat there for a small price. The cook took pity on me; I had no bowl, and he offered me his. He was collecting money in it, so he dumped the money into his pocket, poured the dirt out of the bowl, and banged it against the table a couple of times. He poured some soup into it and handed it to me. I ate it all, even though the last couple of bites were a little gritty.

Before we left Aswan, I met a guy at the youth hostel who was throwing away a foam rubber pad. I took it and used it on the floor of that lounge. Before we went to bed, the Nubians traveling with us gathered around a fire on the deck of the barge. They began singing these chants, which they all knew. One of them would sing a verse, and they would all clap and sing the choruses.

With the Africans singing, we sailed up the Nile in the dark, the desert on both sides, not a light to be seen in any direction, and the stars seemed to come right down to us. I tried to sing along, keeping the tune without the words. It was a magical night and seemed as if it had been arranged for these gentle people to slowly introduce us to the Sudan and black Africa.

We were awakened the next morning at dawn by the Arabs at prayer. They pray five times a day on their knees. You can say what you will about their beliefs, but you can't fault their devotion. As we sailed up the Nile, we could see that it was becoming Lake Nasser. It will take ten years to fully fill in the lake. The wind was cold on deck, and the voyage took four days. We passed the temple of Abu Simbel, which I visited before. The barges never stop there because technically, we'd already left Egypt. I was glad I got to see it up close before I left Egypt.

A makeshift immigration and customs post met us under a tent at Wadi Halfa. A doctor checked our immunization records, but he just looked at the front of mine, never opened it. We changed money, filled out an endless supply of forms, and cleared customs. Some Land Rovers were waiting to take us to the train station. The driver wanted five pounds, which seemed high, but they said, "Long way, mistah. Long way."

Although there wasn't another train for a week, I wanted to save money and started to walk. As we walked up the sand dune in the direction of the station, they would come roaring past us, reducing the fare with each trip. Finally, at the top of the sand dune, we could see the station in the valley maybe a kilometer away. Still, the drivers tried to get a fare out of us. Each time they passed, they reduced the fare: four pounds, three pounds, two pounds, until it was comical to them too.

At the station, we prepared to board the train when we saw a large group of Arabs in a big circle with one man kneeling in the middle. They were singing and chanting, sounding to my American ears like American Indians singing their native songs. As they chanted, they would walk around in a circle. One of them was slinging holy water at the travelers, who smeared it all over their face and chest.

Some of it hit me, and I joined right in smearing it on; they loved it. We learned that they were sending one of their own off on his pilgrimage to Mecca. Finally, everyone was on board, and we set off across the desert to Khartoum.

We immediately realized we should have paid more for a higher class (come to think of it, there probably wasn't a higher class) or at least bargained a little to be more toward the front of the train. As the train picked up speed, the sand billowed around the cars and into the open windows. We had to hold cloths in front of our mouth and nose just to breathe.

It was miserable, so we went to the back of the car and found the ladder to climb up on top. Up there, we were above the billowing sandstorm. It was hot in the desert in January but still better than the dust storm. Somewhere in one of my albums, I have a photo of the silhouette of a train on the desert floor with absolutely nothing else to see in the picture, except lots of sand in every direction. On top of the silhouette of the train is a tiny figure of a man, waving his hand at the camera. That's me!

When it was time to sleep, I put the foam pad up in the luggage rack and climbed up on top of it to sleep. That worked fine until a bloodshot-eyed Arab came screaming in the car about midnight, selling clothes. Toilet facilities on the train were small cabins in the middle of the car with two porcelain footpads and a big hole in the middle. You could see the ground rushing by underneath us.

A funny thing (not so funny at the time) happened on the train. A little old Nubian lady, the wife of a Bedouin, decided it was time for tea. Every day at this time, she fixed her husband tea. She had never been on a train, but she got some sticks out of her bag, built a fire, and started heating the water. Of course, the floor of the train was made of wood, so what happened when she built a fire? It burned down the train car! The train engineer had to disconnect that car and let it burn up, reconnect the rest of the train, and carry on toward Khartoum. (No fire brigade out there!)

That's what made the trip two and a half days instead of one. I can't remember what we ate those two days or even if we ate at all. The life of a vagabond, following the crowd in the direction we were going and doing what they did: eating, sleeping, and traveling together. As we approached Khartoum, stopping at little towns, there were three people sitting in space for two. After thirty-two hours of it, I had enough of Sudanese trains.

The Sudan is the boundary between Arab and black Africa on the eastern side of the Sahara. In the north, it's desert and Arab and Muslim. In the south, it's jungle and black Africans and tribal superstition. The two parts of the country were at war, two cultures trying to coexist. The Arabs control Khartoum, the government, the oil, and therefore, all the money. I had heard from other travelers that if I could get to the south of the Sudan, the African tribes were very friendly and loved to see foreigners; the way the other traveler put it was, "They'll carry you around on their shoulders, mate!" Unfortunately, with the war going on, it just wasn't something I wanted to risk. A year in Vietnam was enough.

In my journal on January 6, 1973, I wrote:

> Now I really feel like I'm in Africa. The people here are very visibly marked by tribal initiation on their faces and bodies and although they still mostly wear the Muslim clothes, they are tall, thin, and very, very black.

On arrival in Khartoum, I found a youth hostel. Because it was a crossroads for those traveling both north and south, there were always people passing through, willing to share travel information about where they'd been and seek information about where they were going. We learned a lot about how to get to where we wanted to go cheaply and gave info about where we'd been—a fair trade.

Khartoum, the capital, is surrounded by desert on all sides with the Nile running through it. One of my theories is that the sophistication of a country is inversely proportional to the amount of bureaucracy needed to travel through it. To travel through Europe, all you do is go get on a plane—no immigration, customs, forms to fill out, visas required, lines to stand in, exit permits, payments, or bribes to make to enter or leave. In the Sudan, we had to do all that and more. The bureaucracy was stifling. It's designed that way so that you must pay someone a bribe. I was loathed to pay a bribe every time I turned around, so I soldiered on through the bureaucracy.

There was a series of agencies to visit, from whom you got stamps and approvals. You had to do the visits to these agencies/offices in the right order and get the appropriate stamps and pay the appropriate amounts, or else you had to start over and do it all again in the right order. It was time-consuming. Many times, we'd arrive at one of these offices to learn that they were closed for the afternoon rest, so we had to come back another day. So I had to stay in Khartoum a lot longer than I would have liked. It is a smelly, dirty, poor city without the necessary transport services like buses or trams. It was hard to get around and even harder to crack the bureaucratic morass.

Of course, just about when you're ready to give up on a place, something wonderful happens to change your mind. I was eating breakfast at a coffee shop. When I went to pay for my coffee and baklava, the lady at the counter said my bill was already paid. Surprised, I asked her who had paid for me. She pointed to a man in a suit standing by himself. I went over to thank him for the breakfast, and he told me an amazing story. His country had sent him to the University of Wisconsin to study engineering. While he was in Madison, some families took him in and left him with a very good feeling about America. He was just returning the favor. He would not let me pay. He wanted me to pay it forward.

And it continued to happen. Leaving the train station one time, a guy offered me a ride. When he dropped me off, he said he'd be back to pick me up and take me to my next destination. I didn't pay much attention and found another ride. Later, as I walked down the street, he pulled up to the curb and chastised me for not waiting for him, a genuinely friendly and helpful guy.

Another time, a guy picked me up, and when I asked him where he was headed, he said, "Never mind. I'll take you where you want to go." He had relatives in the States and just wanted to give me a hand.

That friendliness continued the whole time I spent in Khartoum. One day, while hitching to town from the youth hostel, I was picked up by Anatoly, an officer in the Russian Army and advisor to the Sudanese Army. He was on a two-year posting from Russia. I was tempted to tell him I had been an officer in the US Army, but I thought better of it. In Vietnam, they were funding the other side!

So the visit to Khartoum was marked by frustrating, interminably long bureaucratic hassles and memories of some of the nicest, kindest people you could ever meet anywhere. By now, it was January 11, 1973, and with my Ethiopian and Kenyan visas in hand and all the other stamps and payments made, it was time to leave. My intention was to catch a ride from Khartoum across the desert to the border of Ethiopia. Every day at dawn, the trucks line up on the east side of Khartoum, preparing for the all-day journey across the desert.

We bargained with a few drivers and settled in on a truck, loading our stuff in the back. When the trucks were loaded, they all started across the desert at breakneck speed, maybe twenty-five trucks driving abreast of each other. As the faster trucks moved ahead and created a cloud of dust, the others moved sideways to avoid the dust cloud, and within a few miles, there were dust clouds as far as you could see in either direction.

Our driver was very aggressive. He only had two speeds: stop and go. In go mode, he had his foot pressed all the way to the floor, and the engine screamed as we barreled across the desert. Of course, with no roads and only following dirt tracks, we would come to the odd depression or creek bed. That's when he would go into the stop mode, slamming on the brakes until we bounced through whatever obstruction was in our way, and then it was pedal to the metal again.

I decided very early in this mad rush across the desert to try and get up out of the dust, so I climbed up on top of the cab of the truck, where there was a luggage rack and the driver's personal stuff. I found a bag that worked well as a saddle, and as we hurtled across the desert, I sat astride my saddle with my Vietnam boonie hat on, wearing Levi's and cowboy boots.

At one point, another truck seemed to want to overtake us, and all the people in our truck were cheering our driver to beat the other guy and shouting taunts at the people in the other truck. It was as if these two modern-day stagecoaches were crossing the wilderness. I was up on top in front of our stagecoach, and so I began to shout, "Hyahh, hyahh!" to spur our horses on to beat the other coach. The people in our truck really got into it and started egging me on, and so for the next several miles, we had some fun in a diabolical truck race across the Sudanese desert.

Alongside me up there were two others, one on each side. One was Norbert, one of the French guys with whom I'd been traveling; the other was a Muslim guy from Khartoum. As we traveled, the Muslim guy started working on me like an evangelist for Allah. Couldn't I see that all the other religions of the world were false? And couldn't I see that Muḥammad was the one true prophet of the world? And so on, all day long. I must have agreed with him and been converted to Islam several times that day. Until then, I didn't realize just how evangelistic Muslims could be.

About every three hours, the driver would stop, get down from the truck with his prayer rug, figure out the direction of Mecca, and say his prayers. The rest of us would stand around in the shade of the truck, staying out of the hot sun. At noon, he stopped at a small shack in the middle of nowhere. The other Arabs got some bundles down from the back of the truck, which looked like tablecloths with the four corners tied up. They spread the cloths out in the sand, and in the middle were large bowls of mushed up food they were going to eat.

The rest of us stood around watching all this when one of them invited me to join them. Eduardo, the Brazilian, said, "If a man eats this food, he will not live twenty-four hours more!" I thought I'd give it a try, though, so I tried to mime that I had to wash my hands first. I went inside the little shack, and there was a barrel full of water. I dipped my hands in, and all hell broke loose. They were on me like I had committed the unpardonable sin, yelling in Arabic and pushing and shoving me around. I realized just a little too late that this was the only drinking water within several hundred square miles! It was precious, and I had just dipped my dirty hands in it to wash.

Well, we got past that, and as I sat down on the cloth to take some pita bread with my left hand and dipped it in the bowl, there were more shouting and shoving and pushing and swearing—only this time, they were angry. I was made to understand that you don't put your left hand in the food bowl. I had put *my dirty hand* in their food! To understand how sensitive an issue this is, you need to know that there's no word in their language for toilet paper. They use their left hand and then wash it afterward, so you never touch anyone or *anything important,* especially food, with your left hand.

I managed to get to my pack amidst all the shoving and shouting and showed them that I write with my left hand and that my dirty hand was the right one. They found this incredible but finally accepted it but made it very clear that I was to keep my damned dirty hand out of their food! It may sound comical now, but at the time, it was scary. I thought I faced the prospect of either having the crap beat out of me, being left out there several hundred miles from anywhere or both. Thank goodness they accepted my demonstrated explanation.

We were on that truck all day, and as the sun set behind us and the night overtook us, it began to get cold. The Sudanese kid spoke English, and so did the Frenchman, and the only song we all knew was "Where Have All the Flowers Gone." We sang it at the top of our lungs with gusto, racing across the desert in the dark. And so, that leads me to how I started this chapter. Feeling after more than a year vagabonding twenty-seven countries in Europe and with Egypt and Sudan behind me, I was finally beginning to sense a purpose to it all.

We arrived in Kassala at the border of Ethiopia and soon found another hostel. We also found a food shop where they had this grapefruit drink that was wonderful. We named it Purple Passion. As we spent our days trying to figure out how to cross the border that was closed, passing the purple passion place, we met some interesting people and saw some interesting things. At the *souk* (the market), there were lots of primitive handmade things that I might have bought if I had a way to carry them or even ship them home.

Maybe the most interesting thing we saw at the *souk* was the Hadendoa Tribe. They were a nomadic tribe of people who lived in the desert, herded cattle, and did not respect any man-made boundaries. They have natural Afro-style hair, very dark skin, with very fine features. They wear long brown galabia robes with black vests, carry long swords, and they *never* smile or show any emotion in public. They migrated around that part of Africa, crossing country boundaries with impunity, and nobody messed with them because they were known to be such fierce warriors and because they just didn't pay attention to anyone but those in their own tribe. We thought about taking their pictures because they were so striking in appearance, but we were discouraged from doing it; you photograph them at your peril.

One of the days there, the two Frenchmen and I got bored and decided to hike to some hills in the distance. (Eduardo said, "I don't bear this weather!" and went back to town.) We walked through palm trees, banana groves, and fields and came to a small village. The huts were made of mud and were round with straw roofs. There were lots of screaming children, and the leader of the group spoke to us in some local dialect and invited us into his hut.

Somehow, the French guys had picked up enough Arabic for simple communication, so they understood when he asked us to sit and eat with them. The floor of the hut was dirt but cleanly swept; the furniture was sparse and handmade. We were served water, candy, meats, and coffee that tasted of ginger and spice. As we sat there, more people of the village arrived to look at the foreigners. It seemed that the man who invited us was the village chief, and all these others were his relatives. It was what I would now call my first real native African experience.

It was the time of a Muslim holiday, and people were supposed to roast a sheep and feast on it. They were also supposed to share it with their neighbors, which we became as we walked through their village. Interestingly, the festival was celebrating the time when God spared Isaac from the knife of Abraham. We learned that it's not only in our Bible. So we met more nice, generous people, most of whom spoke no English but shared what they had with us.

One night, as we were leaving the grapefruit drink place, a man approached me and asked if he could walk me back to the hostel. He said that there was a "stealy boy" over there who had been watching and following us, and the man wanted to make sure we got safely home. Another mealtime, a guy approached us with bug eyes, a dirty galabia, and said in broken English, "One, two three, four, five six seven, eight nine ten. Goodbye." and walked away!

We finally discovered that we were simply not going to legally get into Ethiopia from Kassala overland. The two countries were at war, the border was closed, and we had no choice but to fly, so we grudgingly bought tickets to Asmara, Ethiopia.

Before I close this chapter, I want to preach a little. The experience with the man protecting us from the "stealy-boy" was important. Many Americans travel overseas with fear that lurking around every corner is someone who wants to steal from them or cheat them. In fact, I found that nothing could be further from the truth. For every "stealy boy," there are hundreds of good, honest people who will step up to give you advice and help you along safely.

If you are so fearful that you aren't open to aid that local people offer, you may in fact get robbed because of your own fear. You might just get what you expect. That's not to say you should be trusting of everyone who approaches you, but I learned that I should be open to help that people offer and expect the best from people until they show you otherwise. (And I was just arrogant enough that I thought I could outrun them if there was trouble!) This philosophy would serve me well later in Africa.

CHAPTER 9

"This is a Living Theater!"

Before, I described my travel from Egypt up the Nile to Wadi Halfa and then by train on to Khartoum. That time in Khartoum was eye-opening for me because it was my first introduction to the corrupt bureaucracies of African countries. And of course, the wild ride across the desert in a goat truck was so memorable as to help me answer the question of why I was there. The truck across the desert took all day and dropped us in Kassala, Sudan.

As we waited for our flight from Kassala, Sudan, to Asmara, Ethiopia, an old African lady who had tickets on this flight had failed to reconfirm her flight. The steward who was checking documents was taking a hard line and refusing to let her board. She threw a screaming, crying, native fit right there in line. She wailed that she had to get to Asmara, and she couldn't wait another week for the next flight, a matter of life and death (all this being translated for me by the man next to me). Finally, the steward relented, and then she started thanking him with more wailing and shouting, hugging his body, his knees, kissing his shoes—quite a show and another example that every day in Africa was a new day!

Just before the plane departed, the immigration people came on and dragged me off because I had failed to properly get the right stamps in the right places. I was tempted to try the wailing fit routine but instead just reasoned with him, and he let me go. Never happier to leave a place.

The flight was interesting because it was my first in Africa and certainly the first over the hills and desert that makes up most of this continent. I saw primitive villages, some mountains, and lots of empty country. The landing was bad; looking through the door to the cockpit, I could see land, then sky, then land again. Lots of sick people all over the plane.

The airport in Asmara was newer than anything I'd seen in the Sudan, and it was an easy entry. Asmara is in Eritrea Province, which has a different culture and people than the rest of Ethiopia. They wanted to secede and become an independent country for some time, but the king, Haile Selassie, the Lion of Judah, wanted to keep them where they were. There was an American army base in Asmara, and it was believed that the Americans were keeping the lid on things. (Now, Eritrea is a different country.)

When I arrived, the army base was a magnet for me. I walked up to the gate and flashed my military ID I'd kept from Vietnam and was waved in. I thought the MP who saw the state of my clothes and beard would deny me entry, but he saw my rank (captain) and let me in. I found the post exchange, had a meal, and looked around. Shocking! After traveling for a year, the last two months of which in Africa, living and traveling with the people, I was disappointed to see the state of the US Army had not changed—same narrow-mindedness, same fear to venture out into the unknown, and same naivety. I got out of there as soon as I could buy some new underwear. I don't remember where I slept or how long I stayed in Asmara, but I do remember the beauty of the Ethiopian women and spent the night with one—yes, I noticed!

I learned from some fellow travelers that the Feast of Timkat (Epiphany) was about to take place in Axum, the home of the Ethiopian Coptic Church. It was supposed to be an authentic view into this culture, so away I went. To get to Axum, I had to take a bus, which proved to be a wild ride. By this time, I was still traveling with the Brazilian guy Eduardo. Foolishly, we expected assigned seats on a modern tour bus. Wrong! When the bus arrived, it was already full. So we waited for the next bus, which was also full, but we boarded anyway. It was a thirty-five-passenger bus with forty-five people on it. By the time we got out of Asmara, they had picked up another twenty. Without a doubt, the most incredible bus ride of my life. As Eduardo said, "This is a living theater!"

On the way, a window fell out, so they roared to a stop, and with much shouting and running around, they retrieved the window and attempted to reinstall it as we roared off again. As the bus careened around the mountain curves on skinny little roads, the tread on one of the tires came loose, so once again, we slammed to a stop. They cut the separated tread away, and off we went again, only to stop in another twenty minutes to change that tire, which was completely flat by this time.

We stopped several times on this eight-hour trip, and each time we stopped, the bus was completely full, and they took on more passengers. People were sitting in the aisles, on the engine, on the steps, hanging out the door, on top of the bus, and on top of each other. There was alternately someone standing, sitting, kneeling, crouching, and squatting between my legs. There was sleeping, staring, shouting, fighting, and singing. There were men and women with rings in the top and bottom of their ears, in their noses and cheeks. There were towels wrapped around heads, cornrows on the young women, and lots of ritual, tribal tattoos.

What I remember most about this trip was its *invincibility.* No matter what happened on or around that bus, it would make it to the destination. No less than five or six things happened along the way that would have severely interrupted or stopped a trip anywhere else but Africa. Here, it was all in a day's work; everyone took it all in stride, as if they expected this kind of adversity in their everyday lives, and I think they did.

Arriving in Axum, I was approached by a young boy who had a sister with a room she'd rent me for one dollar. I took it, and in the middle of the night, the sister knocked on the door to retrieve her shoes(?). The next morning, a boy walked into the room when I was still sleeping and told me to hurry up because the procession was starting soon. When I walked out of the hotel, I saw the following things just by turning my head: a little girl was taking a dump in the ditch, a man was threatening another man with a rock, a group of men were bowing to each other in the middle of the road, a boy was shining a well-dressed man's shoes, and a huge Brahma steer wandered through it all, oblivious. Welcome to Africa; the living theater continues.

The ceremony began by the Bath of the Queen of Sheba. The priests dressed in elaborate and very colorful costumes walked out of a big tent and up to the top of the dike and began a religious ritual. The chanting and swaying of the people and the high-pitched trill of the women were very similar to what I'd seen back in Wadi Halfa when we got off the barge from the Nile. There was a little old guy with a trumpet, blowing it like mad with never the same notes in succeeding verses. Young boys holding elaborate and similarly colorful umbrellas shaded the priests. There were huge crosses, an arc like the arc of the covenant, and a huge Bible carried by the head priest.

After the ritual ceremony, they all marched down to the lake, and after a helper stirred away the green gunk at the edge of the water, the high priest blessed the water, and three candles were lit and floated out into the lake. When the candles sunk, it was the signal for everyone to start splashing water on everyone else and washing in it.

At the end of all this, a crazy man appeared from somewhere and began admonishing the crowd loudly to be careful and not fall into the water because it was bewitched or something. The police showed up and chased him off, and the procession moved down to the church, stopping occasionally for more chanting, dancing, and drum beating. It was singularly the most incredible religious event I had ever witnessed in my life. Unbelievable!

Leaving Axum, we squeezed onto another already-full bus. At one of the stops, the bus driver said, "Follow me," down a small alley into a small hut. The hut was full of bees buzzing around. We sat down on small mud benches carved into the wall of the hut. Soon, a woman served us a yellow liquid called *tedgeh* or honey wine. The lady serving looked different somehow, and when she served me, I noticed little hands and feet sticking out of her shawl. I learned that all mothers carry their babies that way, even young girls. The wine was very good if you didn't think very much about how it looked, the bees buzzing around, and the state of the hut. That was Africa; if I was going to worry about all that stuff all the time, I had no business traveling overland across Africa.

After two more stops and a *tedgeh* at each place, I was feeling no pain and really enjoyed the bus ride after that. We arrived in Gorgora that evening, found a hostel, and I took a much-needed nap after all the alcohol. Big mistake. After a meal with a Peace Corps worker we met, we retired back to the hostel and discovered it had no electricity—pitch black. The bed had bugs in it, there were rats running around the floor and ceiling, and I wasn't sleepy because of the nap. Long night.

The next day, we took a boat trip across Lake Tana, a huge lake in the center of Ethiopia. Taking the boat was recommended because the roads around there had bandits and were unsafe, plus it was a different way to travel and very beautiful. The boat stopped several times at remote villages only accessible by this boat. At the third village, we hurried through a meal and back to the boat, only to find that the boat was stopping here for the night.

After another all-day boat ride, we landed in Bahir Dar and met some Americans there and found out more about how to get to the Blue Nile Falls. The White Nile starts in Uganda at Murchison Falls, but the Blue Nile starts here in Ethiopia. I knew I'd regret it if I was this close and didn't go see it, so off we went on another bus. Arriving at the park around the falls, we were told it would cost five dollars to see the falls. Remember that we were averaging about a dollar a day for lodging and not much more than that for food, so we were loath to pay. True to form, we found a boy who would guide us through the bush to see the falls without paying. On the way, we were stopped by an official, who demanded we pay, and I was ready to break down, but Eduardo told him he didn't want to see the Blue Nile Falls five dollars' worth, so he just let us go. It was fantastic with wild monkeys all over the jungle around the falls, which was spectacular.

Next day, another bus ride to Debre Markos. On the bus, we met a high school boy who was going home to his village. He invited us to come with him. Once again, we changed plans, got off the bus in the middle of nowhere, and asked where his village was. We walked about a kilometer on a cow track to a grouping of mud and thatched huts. He introduced us to lots of people and finally to his father, the village head. The father had several wives, each of whom occupied one of the huts.

In the main hut, we sat down for a typical Ethiopian meal of injera and *vod* or *wat*. Injera is a large crepe-type pancake made of millet about fifteen inches across. In the center of the injera was dumped a ladle of the *vod* or *wat* like a stew with veggies and meat. You were supposed to tear off a piece of the injera from the edge and scoop up some of the *wat* to eat it, no utensils. It was very good.

Later, we were taken to the cattle pens and learned that they measure wealth by the number and quality of cows they own. The father and his brother were very wealthy by those standards. We watched them milk some cows and drank some of it. I had heard that some of the cows in Ethiopia had tuberculosis, so I feared it but simply could not refuse without offending them.

As the sun set, they walked us back out to the road, protecting us from what they said were hyenas and other wild animals. It was an interesting peek into life in a traditional Ethiopian village, which we would not have had if we were not willing to get off the bus with that kid.

In Addis Ababa, which we reached a couple of days later, I was struck by the beauty of the eucalyptus trees lining the roads into town. King Selassie had visited Australia some time ago and was so taken by the beauty of these trees that he imported enough to line the roads into his capitol, and forty years later, here we were admiring them. I had an experience that first day in Addis that was disturbing: some young men tried to steal my wallet, and a couple of men following me saw what was happening, dragged the thieves around the corner, and beat the crap out of them. Then they came back and apologized on behalf of the Ethiopian people for my inconvenience. Kind of scary but at the same time encouraging, and I still had my wallet!

By the time I reached Addis Ababa, I had been on the road a couple of months without getting funds. The way I did that was to use a credit card as collateral and cash a check at the American Express Bank. In those days, credit cards were only used sparingly and by a few people, and without a job or credit history, I couldn't get one. Mine was a secondary card from my father, so I did not charge with it.

Unfortunately for me, there was no Amex Bank in Ethiopia, and I only had forty dollars left and had to make it to Nairobi, Kenya, before I could access my money. I knew I could barter for transportation or just hitchhike and even sell some of my clothes if necessary, so I wasn't too worried (but I should have been!). I had also heard that about ten hours' drive south of Addis, the hardtop road ended, and it was a two-day trip through the bush to get to the border.

Next day, saying goodbye to Eduardo, I caught a ride to Dilla, ten hours south. That's where the road ended. Standing on the corner, I met a Peace Corps worker who was happy to have an American to talk to. He agreed to let me overnight at his place until I could find a ride south through the bush.

Next day, wandering around downtown, I saw a blond-haired man and went over to talk to him. He was a big game hunter and had just finished an elephant hunt with some wealthy Americans and was headed home to Kenya. He had some large weapons in his truck and was looking for somewhere to get them secured. I told him that if he would give me a ride south, I could help him. I quickly found the Peace Corps worker and arranged for the trucks to overnight in his compound. Over dinner, he learned that I'd been an officer in Vietnam and got very interested in my story. He had idealized war and was sorry he didn't get to participate (really).

We left Dilla at six the next morning, the hunter driving a Toyota Range Rover, his tracker between us and me riding shotgun. His other two trucks followed us. He said a big game hunt would cost about ten thousand dollars. Remember, that this was 1973 and a good salary then was about twelve thousand dollars per year, so this was big money. Their camps were completely self-contained. He had cooks, trackers, mechanics, animal skinners, and laborers to haul everything around.

Midmorning on our first day out of Dilla, we stopped under a baobab tree, and here in the middle of nowhere, the hunter asked if I would like a gin and tonic. I laughingly said that sure I'd like one, plenty of ice. And lo and behold, out of a sophisticated cooler, his servant produced a flask, mixed the drink, and poured it over two ice cubes for me!

That night, the servant put down a ground cloth about twelve by twelve feet, put up a folding cot, put a mattress on it with clean white sheets and blanket for the cold night, and a mosquito net. The hunter said that a hyena won't bother a man sleeping under a net because they think it's a solid object. Then he produced a pan of warm water, soap, and a clean towel for me to wash my face and hands before dinner. Dinner was served on a table he set up with real porcelain plates and silver utensils. I was being treated like one of his clients who paid exorbitant amounts of money for this service!

After dinner, the hunter and I talked in front of the campfire over after-dinner drinks. He is out a month on a hunt and then home for a month. He has consulted for the King Ranch in wildlife control. It was a pleasure and honor to get to know this interesting man. Turning in for bed, the servant appeared again with more hot water for me to wash before bed.

At dawn, I awakened, and at the center of the camp, the cook already had toast, coffee, and marmalade out for breakfast. When we stopped for lunch, there were tuna fish sandwiches. The hunter walked away from the trucks and threw part of his sandwich in the air, and a hawk, which he called a *kite*, swooped down and caught it.

At one point, we were driving along, and the tracker, who was barely five feet tall, shouted to stop. He jumped down, and in front of the truck, he pointed at some tracks in the trail and said they were leopard tracks and no more than twenty-four hours old. Incredible! Another time, when we stopped to fix a leaky radiator, the hunter pointed out wildlife in the area: gazelle, dik-dik, wild boar, and even some lion tracks—but sadly, no lion.

By the middle of the second day, we had really run out of anything resembling a road; it took us ten hours to go just seventy-five miles around boulders, through creek beds, moving fallen trees out of the way, and generally traveling along like pioneers.

Finally, after another night being treated like a king and sharing lots of stories about Vietnam, we arrived in Moyale. Thanks to the hunter and his connections, the border crossing was easy, and I found myself in Kenya. Before the hunter disappeared across the savannah, he offered me some money, which I declined, but I did accept a letter of introduction I could use in Kenya if I ran into trouble. What an experience!

CHAPTER 10

WHAT COLOR IS PREJUDICE?

When I left Tony the hunter, I found a survey crew who were surveying for a new road to Nairobi. One was Mauritian, one Frenchman, and a Kenyan with a civil engineering degree. They let me camp with them and over a campfire told some wild tales. Moyale is the end of the road from Nairobi, and since it's so remote, it gets expensive to travel from. The bus ticket was more than I had left and more than I wanted to pay, but hitching was discouraged by the government in favor of the bus fares. So as I was trying to figure this all out, a Kenyan approached me to buy my cowboy boots. It was getting too hot to wear or lug them around and I needed money, but it was comical watching that little man with his pants tucked into those boots strut away.

After another night with the survey crew and some intelligence gathering, I found a trucker who would take me for a small price, but I'd have to meet him outside of town so the bus drivers wouldn't get wise. I found him about a mile out of town around a corner, and when I climbed aboard, there were four Japanese guys already there. I never did learn where they came from because of the language problem, but we managed with hand signals to get along. Arriving in Marsabit, we slept on the porch of a Catholic church because everything was closed by the time we arrived.

Next day, the luck ran out; we waited all day for a ride—nothing. Finally, the following morning, I broke down and bought a ticket on a bus, which the driver said would arrive in Isiolo by the end of the day. Unfortunately, he didn't say *which day*.

A few hours out of Marsabit, the driver stopped to let a woman on the bus. She was from the Samburu Tribe, wore nothing but a small cloth wrapped around her, was adorned with necklaces and earrings, and her hair and body were painted red, the color of the earth. As the trip progressed, more Samburu, both men and women, got on the bus. The men carried spears and argued hard to bring them on the bus, but the driver insisted the spears had to ride on top.

When they got off the bus, I made the mistake of taking a picture of one of the women. Her husband got irate and started waving his spear at me. Luckily for me, the bus driver kicked the door shut and roared off down the road, laughing to beat the band. He was glad to be rid of them because they never paid.

At dusk, after a seemingly endless stream of stops and starts, the bus driver stopped in the middle of nowhere. He shut off the engine, and it was clear we were there for the night. When we asked why we weren't going on to Isiolo, he just shrugged and said, "No lights." It got worse: he not only had no lights but the bus also had no alternator or starter either. In the morning we were going to have to push it to get it started.

The other Africans put their bedrolls down under a tree and made ready to sleep. The only building for miles around was a little teahouse, where the owner had tea and bread but nothing else. He said if we wanted food, we could cook it ourselves. I wanted to find a good place to sleep with some privacy, but I feared being left behind in the morning, so I climbed up on top of the bus and slept there.

Sure enough, at dawn, all the passengers got behind or beside the bus and pushed it until it roared to life. Arriving in Isiolo about noon, we found the place energized by a visit of President Kenyatta later in the day. As we were eating lunch, all hell broke loose. Policemen came with cane sticks and began to scream at the Kenyans to get out on the street to welcome the president. I stood and looked at them, but they didn't threaten me with the big sticks. Still, I wanted to see this famous man, so I went out on the curb and watched as he slowly drove by. Everyone was waving but clearly not very enthusiastic about it all. I learned that Kenyatta was from a different tribe, and they are still very tribal, not wanting to celebrate another tribal leader.

From Isiolo, I caught a ride to Nanyuki. That's where President Kenyatta is from and his tribe, the Kikuyu, are based. The Kikuyu are very powerful in Kenya because of their connection with the president, who is president for life, not because he is so loved. It's because he disposes of anyone who opposes him. African democracy at its best.

One night, I was walking back to the hostel from dinner and heard loud music coming from an upstairs room. I climbed the stairs and found it full of young people dancing to African rock and roll. I was the only white face in the crowd, which drew some attention, and I ended up paired with a cutie who could really dance as could I. We danced until late and left together.

While we were walking down the street, a police car pulled up and stopped us. They told me I had broken the law, walking with a woman who is not my wife after midnight. I laughed, but they were dead serious. They said they would take us to jail if we didn't pay them a bribe of ten shillings right then. That really pissed me off, so I shot back that they could cuff me and take me to jail, no bribes! But the girl got really upset and asked me to pay them because her father was an important man in town and her getting arrested would be disgraceful. So I paid them reluctantly, and she came back to the hostel and spent the night with me.

Next morning, she was gone, and I thought the worst. But as I walked out to the highway and was waiting for a ride, I heard my name being called and turned around to see her running down the road, waving a ten-shilling bill. She apologized and thanked me for helping her out.

I caught rides from Nanyuki to Nyeri and on to Nairobi the next day. Along the way, we were stopped again for the president's procession. At this place full of Kikuyu, he was revered, and I realized that this tribal culture was something I did not understand. Arriving in Nairobi at night, I was in the first Western-style city for several months, and it was overwhelming. I tried to find the youth hostel the guys in Moyale had told me about, but when I got there, I was turned away—no reservation, no bed. A kid on the street told me I should go to City Park, where there were some people like me camping. Arriving at the entrance to City Park, there was a Dairy Freeze. I got a bite to eat and walked into the park and to a big surprise.

There were two big parking lots at City Park, and in the back one, what I found was a campground full of people like me from all over the world: Americans, Australians, Brits, New Zealanders, Irish, and other Europeans. Some had big trucks they had driven across the desert through the Congo to sell in East Africa. Some had Volkswagen campers, and some had motorcycles, but most, like me, were afoot, just vagabonding around the world. Some had tents, and some like me just slept on the ground. I was suddenly on another trip altogether!

There was a campfire, people playing music, singing, and talking, and of course, lots of marijuana and other stuff. The dope was cheap and plentiful, but I wasn't into it. I didn't smoke, so that was an issue, and I didn't like altering my consciousness because I didn't want to miss an opportunity with the ladies. I climbed into my sleeping bag, listening to music and not feeling so alone.

The next day was washday since I'd been on the road a while, and I continued to get around, making new friends and trying to organize a trip to the game parks. A game warden came around every day to collect camping fees, but it was a joke because he only wanted two shillings from each campsite. So a few of us without tents got a ground cloth and slept under it, claiming it to be our campsite, and so we only paid two shillings every tenth day.

One night around the campfire, I was talking with this Irish guy about the troubles in Northern Ireland. I asked him to explain it to me. He asked me what color prejudice is. I told him where I come from, it's black versus white, but he said, "No, no, no. The color of prejudice is green." He explained that the English were the moneyed class, the businessmen, white-collar guys. The indigenous Irish were the blue-collar, working-class guys who had to work for the English because the English controlled it all. It was all about money. He said that anytime there's prejudice, there's also someone taking advantage of someone else or feeling disadvantaged over money. Since then, anytime I see prejudice, I look for the money; he was right.

Finding this place was both exhilarating and frightening. Exhilarating because there were people like me to talk to and find out about where they'd been and what they'd done. Frightening because there was a tendency to stay there too long, to hide among the people of like minds and not get out and see Africa. It had the potential of becoming kind of a commune, where people live instead of a stopping point on the way. I was so worn out after my travels through Egypt, Sudan, and Ethiopia that I was glad to be there, but I could see that I needed to make plans to leave soon.

On Monday, when the bank opened, I went to American Express and got money. I had made it to Nairobi with less than forty dollars left, so I was relieved to have some travelers checks again. I went to the camera shop downtown where the Indian owner would give me twelve shillings to a dollar instead of the government rate of seven to one. Why? Because the East African governments were making it hard on the Indians, who ran all the commerce, to get their money out. So if they could do black market transactions and get hard currency, they were happy, and the travelers were happy too. As I traveled through all East Africa and further south, I learned that the merchants of East Africa are all Indians.

I went to the post office and collected mail I'd had forwarded there. In those days, there was a system called poste restante, where you could have mail forwarded for you to pick up when you arrived. I wrote in my journal while enjoying some downtime in Nairobi that I was discovering a lifelong quest to travel the world. I was learning that there are too many places to see and things to do to get it all in during one trip around the world.

The more I see and learn, the more I *want* to see and learn. When I find a place worth visiting, I learn about three more. I would run out of money and need to space out my travel during my lifetime to see it and see it well. That led to thoughts of what to do next. I decided to apply to some graduate schools for the following school year, that I would travel the rest of Africa and then head back home. It was partially a factor of running out of my savings from Vietnam and partially just a desire to go home, get my life on track, and then hit the road again when the time is right. I might as well get the education behind me, get a job where I'll make the kind of money that will free me to pursue this travel quest more and more.

While in downtown Nairobi, I went to a leather shop and bought leather and tools to make myself a passport case to wear on my belt. I had done some leather work in the past and knew I could do it with the right tools and time. I went back to City Park and sat under a tree, and while I was working, people passing by would see my work and ask me to make them a passport case. Without meaning to get into the case-making business, I made several of them until I was ready to move on.

The big attraction in East Africa then and now is the game parks. People came there to see the African animals in the wild. In City Park, everyone had either been around the game parks or were planning it. I met a couple named Dave and Sharna from Connecticut and Don from Denver, who had just split with his girl, and we agreed to do the game parks together. We went to a place downtown and rented camping gear—tents, lanterns, etc.—and then went to a car rental place and rented a cheap car (nine shillings a day and sixty-five cents a mile) for a week. We would first go to Amboseli National Park, then into Tanzania and see Arusha, then Olduvai Gorge where the Leakeys were discovering the origin of our species. After that, we would go to the Ngorongoro Crater, drive across the Serengeti plain, and cross back into Kenya.

The first thing that happened was Dave disconnecting the speedometer so we would not have to pay the mileage. Next, even though I had driven on the left side of the road, when you're out in the middle of nowhere, it's hard to remember when you turn right to go to the left lane. We topped a hill, and there was someone in my lane. I was about to give him hell when I realized it was me in the wrong lane. Wake-up call!

We stumbled into the Amboseli campground late, and our first night using the new camping gear was a disaster. We did manage to light the lantern and leave it on all night so the predatory cats and hyenas would stay away. The next day, we followed a Swedish photographer around and saw animals, lots of animals from zebra to elephant, gazelle, ostrich, giraffe, cape buffalo, and more wildebeest than you could count. In the afternoon, we saw a rhinoceros. The Swedish guy's guide admonished us to be quiet. Rhinos are nearly blind and very stupid. They hear their own droppings and turn and charge, so they could to a lot of damage to our car, not to mention to us if we attracted their attention. Finally, that day, we found a cheetah sunning herself on a knoll, a beautiful animal.

The following morning, we heard noises outside our tent, and when we looked outside, there was an elephant pulling leaves off the tree we were camped under. We spent some more time there and crossed over into Tanzania and Arusha National Park. There we saw hippos for the first time and many other animals before heading to the Lake Manyara Lodge. It's on a hill, and using binoculars, you could look down at all the animals coming to drink at the lake. From there, we drove to Ngorongoro Crater National Park. There was a beautiful lodge where the rooms and food were very expensive, so we went to the driver's restaurant and ate the very good local food for a fraction of the lodge prices.

Next day, we went down into the crater, which you must do in a Land Rover accompanied by a guide. It is a self-contained natural setting known to have a perfect balance of nature. There were predators for each type of animal and plant, and they all lived in harmony. It's a great place to go if you only have one place to go because every type of animal in Africa is present in the crater, and we saw them all.

From Ngorongoro, we went to Olduvai Gorge, the place where the Leakey family had found the oldest skeletal remains of man, supposedly three million years old. We met some of the family, and they educated us a little, but we were more interested in seeing the migration, so we hightailed it for the Serengeti. In March each year, the wildebeest and zebra migrate across the Serengeti, following the water. There were literally millions of them moving and being followed secretly by predators, who pulled the old and infirmed out of the herd and ate them.

We spent the night at Seronera, where we camped and cooked our evening meal. We had been told to be sure and clean up our cooking pots and utensils after eating because they would attract hyenas. We slipped up that night, and in the morning, we found our pots scattered all around.

At Seronera, Don, the lawyer from Denver, decided to go with some other people, and a girl named Sondra joined our group. We drove on to the western side of the Serengeti to a place called Fort Ikoma, another resort. Fort Ikoma was run by an American guy who befriended us and let us use the pool and hang around the lodge. After a good swim, we drove to the campground, set up camp, and as usual, found the driver's restaurant.

While we were there, the lights went out for a while, and when we got back to the car, it had been ransacked. My little Swiss backpack was gone, and in it was my passport, all my traveler's checks, and my movie camera. I was sick with anger and loss. I was also afraid of what we would do next because the nearest US passport office in Tanzania was in Dar es Salaam at the other end of the country.

Skip, the American guy running the resort, told me not to worry. He gave me a letter in an envelope and told me to give the letter to the border guard when we went back into Kenya, which was much closer than driving all the way down south. We drove up to the border station, and I handed the *letter* to the guard. When he opened the envelope, a twenty-dollar bill fell out. He smiled and waved us through.

Back in Nairobi, we dumped all our stuff at City Park and returned the car and the camping gear. I then began the job of replacing my passport and money. I went to the US Embassy, and they said yes, they could replace the passport; just give them forty dollars. I explained that my money had all been stolen too, and they said to go to Amex and replace the traveler's checks and come back. At Amex they said yes, they could replace the T-checks, just show them the passport. Grrrrr! A classic catch-22.

The bank manager heard the raised voices and came out to see what was happening. He just smiled and pulled out his wallet; he gave me forty dollars, told me to go get my passport, and come back and pay him back with the replaced T-checks. What a nice guy!

Within the hour, I was back in City Park, new passport and traveler's checks in my new passport case, and all was well with the world.

We arrived back in City Park, Nairobi, later that day and said goodbye to Sharna and Dave. I was now ready to move on. Before we went around the game parks, I met a young lady who wanted to see Southern Africa, but her sister wanted to travel with some English guys. Her name was Ruthi from Oregon, age nineteen and beautiful, and she was still in Nairobi when we returned.

We decided to take a trip to the coast of Kenya, Mombasa, and Malindi and see if we were compatible travel companions. We caught a ride to the coast with the English guys from London who were fun loving, although perpetually stoned. We had a great time on the coast sleeping on the beach and angering the English lady who owned the resort above the beach.

Walking around downtown, I met a guy who had just arrived on a ship from India. I told him I was thinking about taking that boat to Bombay someday. He looked me up and down and said I wasn't ready for India! He said that in India, you either go with lots of money to get above the madness or blend in and get along. His perception of me was that I was in neither category. Something to think about. Mombasa was a big dirty city, so we were quick to move on.

In Malindi, we got a room in a posh hotel and later went to a dance there. All the others staying there and dancing were English people who were very traditional in English dress and custom. We sort of stood out in our hippie clothes. After Malindi, we went north to Lamu Island. On Lamu, we stayed at a lodging called "the Castle," which was a hippie dive in the center of town. I remember a sign in the restaurant selling *geoget*—huh? I figured out that it was their way of spelling yoghurt.

We spent a few days there, swimming naked in the ocean, climbing the sand dunes, and eating seafood overlooking the bay. It was magic, and Ruthi and I were getting along well. One day, I think I had an allergic reaction to some of the seafood. My upper lip began to swell to twice its normal size. I went to a clinic and got an antihistamine shot, which brought it down, but the magic of Lamu was over for me. Time to go.

On the way back to Malindi, the bus slipped off the road because of the heavy rain. Everyone piled off the bus, pushed it back up onto the road, and away we went again. We caught easy rides back to Mombasa and then the overnight train back to Nairobi. That train ride is worth describing. When we boarded, there was a wild-eyed guy who'd been chewing *murungi*, a hallucinogenic weed, singing loudly, and he was still singing fifteen hours later when we arrived in Nairobi.

There was a toothless old black lady sitting across from us, staring at us—for fifteen hours! We went to the dining car and sat with an American man who, it turns out, was the Peace Corps director for Malawi. Great meal, nice conversation, and a chance of meeting up with him when we went south to Blantyre.

Back in Nairobi, there was a huge rain, and the campground was soaked. I decided to do something completely different, so I went to the New Stanley Hotel, one of the nicest there, and got a room. I went back to City Park and told everyone if they wanted to get out of the rain, they could come to the hotel for a nice hot shower; the only cost to them was to bring some food. We had twenty-seven showers in twenty-four hours, and I was the hit of the Park.

I also called my parents, with whom I had not spoken in months, and dropped the news that the hotel bill was going on the Amex card. (I later learned that my mother had called the State Department. because she was worried about me. The officer put her on hold and then came on the line to tell her I was not in jail in Africa! They keep records of that, but it was little consolation to her.)

At the New Stanley Hotel, some of us went to the restaurant, and one guy ordered a BLT. It didn't come out of the kitchen right, and the guy let the poor waiter have it. Now, here is a guy only fifteen years after independence, before which he would not be allowed on the porch of that hotel. He was listening to us in a foreign language, trying to understand what a BLT was, which he'd never tasted in his life and serving foreigners who didn't even speak the same English he'd been taught. I thought, *We should be happy we got anything resembling a BLT and not cow's blood or something else common to them.* And it was right then I decided it was time to go. Ruthi said goodbye to her sister, we called Ruthi's mom to assure her I would take care of her, and we got ready to go. We removed our belongings from City Park and started catching rides south. South Africa, here we come!

CHAPTER 11

"*Poli, Poli, Mistah!*"

After the trip to Mombasa and Lamu with Ruthi, we were both getting comfortable with each other. Her sister was with us most of that time, but when we got back to City Park in Nairobi, she decided she wanted to go back to England with one of the Cockney guys. Ruthi wanted to go south. Since they had promised their mother they would not split up, we went to the post office and called their mother in Oregon. We talked it through, and I promised her I would take care of Ruthi and not abandon her in some godforsaken place, and she reluctantly gave her blessing to us traveling to South Africa together. The sisters had promised their mom that they would come back to Oregon together, so they agreed to meet up again in England in a few months and travel home together.

Ruthi and I left City Park on the third of April 1973. We took the number 13 bus to the airport; three quick rides later, we were in Arusha, Tanzania, checking into the Continental Hotel for seven and a half shillings a night (about 0.75 dollars). The funny little guy that gave us a ride to Arusha really amused me. He had a tape deck in the car that I was obliged to hold on my lap, and as we began the drive, he flipped it over, and I'll be damned—it was a Jim Reeves tape of sickly sweet very country music. There we were driving through the African bush with a Kikuyu Kenyan guy, one generation off the tribal village, in a British car, listening to American country and Western music, and watching giraffe nibbling the tops of the trees as we drove by. Heck of an experience for an uprooted Okie!

Next day, we caught a quick ride for about ten miles with an American veterinarian doing work for the Tanzanian government, and then as I was beginning to think we were in for a long wait, the first car passing by picked us up. That experience was repeated time after time as Ruthi stood out on the side of the road with her pretty all-American blond looks and charmed her way all the way to Johannesburg.

Arriving in Moshi, Tanzania, we were approached by a Swiss couple who wanted us to climb Kilimanjaro with them. While at City Park, we had met many people who either had climbed or were preparing to climb the big mountain. It's the highest peak in Africa, nineteen thousand feet altitude. I was thinking I didn't really care about doing it because it had become "the thing to do." But the Swiss couple's enthusiasm was infectious, and we eventually agreed to go up with them.

We spent some time researching it and learned that most people hire a guide to show them the way up and carry their gear, but that was a little expensive. It was possible to do it without a guide, and we met several people like us who had done it. We also learned that it was very cold up there, so we had to rent some more clothes and warm sleeping gear. We also had to carry food for five days.

The Swiss were named Rudi and Frennie, a married couple who had been working in South Africa for a few years. They had bought an old Volkswagen van and fixed it up and were planning to drive it back home to Switzerland. Since they had done some climbing in the Alps, we thought it was a good idea to climb with them since neither Ruthi nor I had any experience mountain climbing. We rented gloves, masks, long johns, and bought some canned food and went to bed in their tent, excited about the climb the next day. Mosquitoes ate me up that night, and I didn't sleep well. That lack of sleep caused me to almost give it up that first day of climbing.

We drove to the hotels (which were at about six thousand-foot altitude) at the foot of the mountain and parked there to start the hike up. There are three huts where most people pace themselves to reach each day on the way up and then take two days hiking down, five days in all. The first day was the toughest, one endless stretch of walking after another. The hike starts at the hotels, and the first hut I think is at about nine thousand feet but a long walk.

The first three to four miles, we saw Tanzanians who live in little villages along the path. One lady was walking up to her village with a fifteen-day-old baby; imagine someone in this country hiking up a mountain fifteen days after giving birth! We hiked what seemed like all day, and when we arrived at what I thought was the first hut, I was glad to be there because I was whipped, only to learn that we were only halfway there! We hiked and hiked and hiked, and I stopped several times, carrying a heavy pack, and asked myself, "Why am I doing this?"

When we finally did arrive at the first hut, I got chills and other bad reactions (which I now understand as dehydration), and I thought to myself, *If I don't feel any better tomorrow than right now, Kilimanjaro will be a dream, forever.*

The morning brought a new day! My legs support my body (surprise!). We hiked from hut number 1 through a rain forest of dense overhanging trees and thick underbrush—moss hanging down from all the trees, a surreal environment. We got our first good look at Kilimanjaro as we exited the rain forest; it looked far away still. We passed through three hours of rolling hills and gradual uphill grades. We were hurrying to get to hut number 2 because we had heard it rains every day near there. The flowers on these hills and vistas from the hills made me think about just staying there and not being part of the Tanzanian Tourist Board's herd up the hill. It would have been so nice to just camp there among those flowers for a few days and enjoy the peace and quiet.

We pressed on to hut number 2 and arrived at 3:00 p.m. just before the rain. Rudi and Frennie are a matched pair. He starts the stove, and she starts to prepare the food, and their actions complement each other, working together until it's time to eat. They eat, and then the work resumes, with each of them doing their part of the cleanup until it's done. At first, we tried to help with this process, but that seemed to throw them out of their routine and confuse them. So eventually, we just sat back and watched the scene unfold until it was time to dish up the food. Then after we ate, we sat back again and watched the scene resume to completion.

After dinner, we went outside and looked down from our perch at the twelve-thousand-foot level of Kilimanjaro and watched a thunderstorm from above! We could see the clouds below us and the rain falling from the clouds below, and then occasionally, lightning would come out of the cloud below us and go down into the rain. It was eerie.

We struck out the third day from hut number 2, and after hiking about two hours, we arrived at one side of a saddle. We could see hut number 3 from there, across on the other side of the saddle. We made the mistake of eating some lunch before striking out across the saddle, and it made us all sick. We later learned that if you're not used to the altitude, eating can make you nauseous. We hiked across the saddle and up to hut number 3, Kibo Hut, arriving at 3:00 p.m. again. We had nothing to do but sit around and feel sick.

The 15,500-foot altitude was affecting all of us, so after nibbling a little food and feeling ill again, we climbed into our sleeping bags. It was also very, very cold. A white Zambian couple also arrived at the hut with their son and a guide. The Zambian was a racist, with some racial slur to liven every conversation, and I disliked him. But he did have a guide and was going to make the final ascent at 2:00 a.m. because he wanted to be at the summit at dawn, and apparently, that's when the oxygen is the best.

During the night, I would fall asleep, but my normal breathing pattern wasn't sufficient to give me enough oxygen at sixteen thousand feet, so I would awaken, gasping for air. This went on all night.

The guide banged on the door at 1:00 a.m. with tea and cookies, and we shivered into our clothes. Ruthi and Frennie couldn't make the big step out of bed. Both were still really feeling the altitude sickness. I put on my gloves and Ruthi's and all the rest of the clothes I could wear and struck out behind the Zambian and his guide. The guide had a lantern, and he slowly marched up the mountain, chanting, "Poli, poli. Poli, poli" (slowly, slowly). It seemed like two steps forward and one step back on the gravel path. It was very dark and very cold, and I was dizzy and hallucinating goofy dreams in the darkness. I dreamed about arriving at the top and running around and then sliding down the other side into Kenya and being heralded for finding a new route up Kilimanjaro.

As we climbed, the Zambian bigot, as I had christened him, started harassing poor Rudi about sniffling too much and not using a hanky! In almost any other place on this planet, I would have throttled the jerk, but in this semiconscious state, staggering up a steep gravely mountain path, it was all I could do to just put one foot in front of the other. We were an odd assortment: A Zambian bigot, a little Swiss mouse of a guy, an itinerant Okie, and a Tanzanian black man who had done this 457 times before, and the only thing making this significant was that it was the 458th.

I was in the back of the group. The others in front of me were struggling too—two steps and slide—and that broke the rhythm of the climb for me. So I would stop and catch my breath, and then in the darkness, I'd go straight for the light of the lantern. That took me off the path and made for harder climbing, which made me stop more, a repeating bad cycle. I started getting dizzy from the exertion and the altitude and falling. It was also very cold, negative fifteen degrees centigrade.

From there on, I really don't remember how we got to the top or how long it took. The Zambian was bitching about having to stop and wait for me, but the guide knew better than to leave someone near the top of a nineteen-thousand-foot mountain, dizzy and lost. It's all a blur from then until I got back to hut number 3.

We did make it to the top at a little before dawn and watched the sun come up from the top of the world! It was a 360-degree sunrise; that much, I do remember. To enjoy the sunrise, all I had to do was sit and watch. Here's what I wrote about it then:

> The sun turned the clouds on the horizon more colors of red and orange than I could ever imagine. The colors kept changing until everything took on color and the World unfolded below us. It was like watching the creation of a day from heaven, from a totally unaffected vantage point high above it all.

I also remember thinking, *I've come this far. I've signed the book up here.* Once the sun was up, I wanted *down!*

Then the guide, Dowdy, produced some tea from his bag and shared it around. That was all it took for me; I began to throw up from the altitude. It was time to go down, *right now.* On the way down (when I wasn't stopping to puke), the gravel was loose, and I could just point my feet one way and slide, just like on skis, then I made a turn by jumping up and coming down, facing the other way down the slope, and skied down some more. Fun.

When we arrived back at hut number 3, the girls were just getting up, and I remember having to encourage Ruthi to hurry up because I was still feeling sick. I was convinced that the faster I got to a lower altitude, the better I'd feel. It turned out not to be true. Altitude sickness must run its course, and running back down wouldn't have helped.

When we arrived at hut number 2, it was raining, so we stopped there for the night. We had hidden some food there to eat on the way down. We had a meal, and it was only then that I began to feel a little better. Funny thing: it didn't bother Rudi as much. I later thought it must have to do with body fat; he was very lean and much leaner than me. I certainly wasn't heavy but even at 160 pounds. I was heavier than him.

We met some Dutch guys at hut number 2 who climb a lot. They had come from the bottom that day. The following morning, they hiked to hut number 3, left their gear, hiked to the top and back, picked up their gear, and hiked back down the same day. Two days total! They were experienced mountain climbers, but still, I was impressed.

The final day, we hiked from hut number 2 past hut number 1 and on down the mountain. Late in the afternoon, it started to rain one of those African-deluge kinds of rains, and we hid under the eaves of a building. We caught a ride with a passing Land Rover and rode the last three miles to the car park. Rudi and Frennie, in their own Swiss way, had to cook a meal right then and there before taking us back to the town of Moshi. We were tired and annoyed to have to wait on them, but we made it. We had hiked seventy miles in five days, a total twenty-six thousand feet of altitude change in all, up and down. When we arrived back at the YMCA in Moshi, we finally got a shower and a meal and died for the night.

The next day, we returned the rented clothes and gear, washed clothes, read books, and let our sore muscles recuperate a little. The YMCA in Moshi is very good and very cheap and a perfect place for us right then. After our rest day, we were ready for the next part of our adventure. We planned to hitch down through Tanzania. Then, where the main north-south road meets the east-west road from the Zambian copper mines to Dar es Salaam, we would decide whether to go east to Dar es Salaam or west to Zambia. It would depend on whom we met along the way and what they told us about those alternatives.

We were ready to leave the YMCA in Moshi, Tanzania, right after breakfast. Since it was included in our bill, I was sure going to enjoy breakfast, and I did but for a different reason: I met an American woman who was also traveling around who was an ex-nun from an order in New York. She had quit the church because as a teacher, she wanted to use more progressive teaching methods than they could accept, plus she had a hard time with the way they disciplined the kids. It was the first time I had met anyone who had been that involved with the Catholic Church, and it was enlightening talking to her.

Our first ride took us to the junction where the road turns south, and we waited there for a while as all the local cars passed (no one traveling through). Finally, about an hour later, a businessman, Rohan from Nairobi, came along on his way to Tanga. We jumped in with him, and after a few hours' drive, he said he wanted to stop for lunch at a hotel up in the mountains he had heard about. So without any other pressing matters, we accompanied him up this steep mountain road to the Lawns Hotel. On the way, we really saw rural Tanzania, with people living in little mud huts clinging to the sides of the mountain, lush greenery all around, and shambas (small farms) of banana, sisal, and vegetables along the way. There were people walking along the road, digging, tending sheep or goats, or children chopping various plants and always stopping to stare at the foreigners passing by.

Our host at the Lawns Hotel was an Asian gentleman (that's a nice way in East Africa of referring to Indians) who prepared a delicious slow late lunch in the middle of this jungle paradise. By the time we finished lunch, it was already 4:30 p.m., so our driver decided to stay the night there. That put us in a little bind because we had been planning on camping out or staying at a local hotel, where it was very cheap. This place charged 150 shilling a night, so I explained our situation to the manager of the hotel and offered to pay fifty shillings a night. After some haggling, he agreed to let us stay for sixty shillings—after all, the hotel was not full, and sixty shillings was better than nothing.

Our new friend and driver Rohan had lived in East Africa all his life and had some local insights he shared. The Maasai are a warrior tribe of people that live in East Africa. They are nomadic and do not recognize any authority apart from their own tribe. They don't wear clothes, only robes thrown over their shoulder, but they are very vain and wear lots of fancy necklaces, earrings, and other adornments. They move freely between Kenya, Tanzania, and Uganda, herding their cows, which is their measure of wealth. They also take cows from other tribes and families because they believe that all the cows are really theirs in the first place; they see themselves as the chosen people of God.

The other Kenyans are very tolerant of the Maasai, partly because they know they can't change them, and partly because they are afraid of them. In the Kenyan Air Force, when they try to teach the Kenyans to fly, they all do well on the ground training, but when it comes to operating the controls of the plane and getting it off the ground, the Maasai don't have enough courage to move the controls and make it fly. All of this, of course, was courtesy of Rohan.

We also talked about the politics of Tanzania. The government has invited the Chinese in to help them build a railroad from Zambia out to the coast of Tanzania. They had to do this because they don't trade with Southern Rhodesia or South Africa. Also, because of the instability of Mozambique at that time, they can't go that way, so the only way to the port for the copper from the mines in Zambia is through Tanzania.

I would like to take some time explaining something of the history and politics of Southern Africa at the time for you to understand my story better. As I have mentioned before, much of Eastern and Southern Africa were at one time British colonies. Tanzania used to be called Tanganyika, Malawi used to be called Nyasaland, Zambia used to be called Northern Rhodesia, and Zimbabwe was Southern Rhodesia. All this was prior to independence, which happened in the middle of the twentieth century. All those countries, since independence had been taken over by presidents-for-life leaders who had been elected in a quasi-democratic fashion and then killed off the opposition to stay in power. The good news for me was that these countries were very stable and safe to travel.

All these countries, with their independence, had a love-hate relationship with Southern Rhodesia and South Africa. Those countries still had booming economies that employed large numbers of people from the neighboring countries. So the neighboring *free* countries tolerated the racism of apartheid (or separateness) among the races. Mozambique, the country just east of both Rhodesia and South Africa, was a colony of Portugal, and they were in the last stages of a civil war when I was there.

The effect all this had on me was very little, except that in the independent countries, they were all trying so hard to modernize and make it seem just like their ex-rulers, the British. In the countries that were still colonies or white controlled, they spent all their time trying to defend their policies and convince us that they were doing the right thing. Because these countries were basically military dictatorships, it worked in my favor because they were also very stable and easy to travel in once you got past the tyranny of the military and police. Not so stable or safe today—in fact, I don't recommend the trip I did to anyone now.

Rohan was going to Dar es Salaam, the capital of Tanzania, which was east of our turnoff about two hundred kilometers. We decided not to go there and to turn west at the Lushoto junction, which was in between Dar and Tanga, the western-most village in

Tanzania. We waited four hours for another ride and finally realized we were telling people the wrong city name, so they didn't understand and didn't take us. Finally, we hopped on a bus, and the driver straightened me out about the geography.

We stopped in Morogoro for the night and met Blue, or that's what he asked us to call him. He's an Asian boy (Indian) who decided to be our guide while we were there. He is a Sikh who cut his hair and went modern (he said it was two feet long when he cut it). Most Sikhs never cut their hair and wear a colorful turban, which we saw a lot of in East and Southern Africa. Blue took us to a local grease-house café and insisted on buying our dinner.

He talked to us a lot about the situation in his country from his point of view. The Indians are the merchants and professional people of Africa, but on the political scale, they are way down the pecking order. He was a nice kid in his teens, stuck in a small village in Western Tanzania, with dreams of escaping to the US for an education. His folks just tolerated us; they were afraid we'd put crazy ideas in his head, I guess.

All that trouble we had hitching the day before, we attributed to being Friday the Thirteenth, and as if the old myth that good luck follows bad on the Saturday after the thirteenth, we had two of the best rides we'd ever had. The last ride we had was with a guy we called the "Leyland man" because he was a paint salesman from Dar es Salaam. We piled into his Volkswagen bug and traveled all the way to Iringa with stops for coffee at Mikumi Wildlife Lodge, stops for pictures of lion in the park, tea at an intermediate town, and lunch at the Hotel White Horse in Iringa.

The Leyland man dropped us at the Whitehorse Hotel and paid the bill. He had also paid for other expenses that day. When we stopped moving in our hotel room for a minute, I became skeptical of his generosity and waited for the other shoe to drop. He'd been leering at Ruthi all day.

The Leyland Man and a friend picked us up to go to dinner, and the friend kept lording it over the Leyland Man and telling us about his caste until I called him on it, and he admitted that the caste system is only respected among the Indians living there. They were very interested in the US and asked tons of questions about our standard of living and things there while we picked their brains about how things were from their perspective in East Africa. Next day, we all piled into the Volkswagen and went to Mbeya, where we found a room at the Mbeya Railway Hotel, where the food was delicious.

At the hotel, we met a Swiss guy who convinced us that Lusaka, capital of Zambia, was a long way and not worth the trip. He suggested we take a side road over into Malawi, all the way to Lake Malawi. There, we could catch a boat down the lake and basically travel the length of the country, seeing it from the water and enjoying a view of Africa that would be new and refreshing. Another problem if we went down through Lusaka was politics.

Crossing over from Zambia to Southern Rhodesia was iffy at best and sometimes impossible. We didn't want that hassle. Finally, we had heard that South Africa was clamping down on *hippies* arriving there with no money and just existing at the expense of the South African government, so they were requiring that visitors to South Africa have some sort of ticket that would take them back to their home when they arrive in South Africa. Of course, I did not have such a ticket, so I was trying to get around this problem. While in Nairobi, I went to Pan American Airways and bought a ticket from Johannesburg to New York. I waited a few days and then went back and cancelled the ticket but kept the receipt to show the South Africans if asked.

Whenever we met people heading north, we always asked them about the problem of entering South Africa and how to get around it. The Swiss guy just reinforced what we had heard about entering South Africa and told us again that going in through Swaziland was the best way. Swaziland is a small country wedged between Mozambique and South Africa. Its sole claim to fame is the gambling casinos there, where the rich Johannesburgers go to gamble on weekends. If you showed up at the border of Swaziland and South Africa on a Sunday afternoon when there was a line of cars going home, it was supposedly easier to get across the border because they were laxer. More on that later.

CHAPTER 12

"You got your visa in Nairobi but I'm in charge here!"

At the border between Tanzania and Zambia, we were hassled about foreign exchange and then finally got across into Zambia, where it was nice and more modern and cleaner than Tanzania. We met a new traveling companion, Owen, and prepared to travel to Malawi the next day. You've heard me mention different people I met along the way. That's significant because it's important to understand the culture of the time. There were lots of people in their twenties traveling around the world from everywhere you could think of. The more remote you got, the more you saw Aussies and Brits and Canadians. The Americans were also there but in less numbers than in places like Europe.

We were warned that the border crossing between Zambia and Malawi was a long way out in the bush, and we would probably get hassled. The reputation of Malawi was that it was a very conservative place, where vagabonds like us usually had trouble. Before we left on the bus, the police pulled me off the bus, and after some confusion, I realized that they had caught a guy going through Ruthi's bags. He was caught red-handed with some cigarettes we had bought to use for trade, and after I signed a statement, he was marched off to jail.

The bus trip was the usual chaotic African scene. At the Zambian side of the border, the bus conductor and the customs guy had a big argument, and everything had to be taken down off the top of the bus for inspection. Before we arrived in Malawi, I got Ruthi to lop off about four inches off the back of my hair so that I looked a little more respectable.

On the Malawi side, where we expected to be hassled, it was smooth sailing, except for one immigration guy. He said, "You got your visa in Nairobi, but I am in charge here, and the visa is no good if I don't say it's good." By this time, I had learned a little about how to operate in Africa; back to the time and money idea: with infinite time, it takes less money. He thought I was in a hurry to get going and I would be prepared to pay him a bribe. However, if I just waited him out and had enough patience, it would happen without the bribe, so I did not even pretend to understand why the visa was no good and just continued in a calm voice to insist that his country would not have issued a visa that was no good. His eyes had the bloodshot look of too much African beer, and I could see that he was fading. Finally, he went and sat down and fell asleep, and one of the other guys stamped my visa, and away we went. Of course, the bus driver wouldn't leave me, so he too was pushing to get going.

I asked the second immigration guy if I really needed to cut my hair, and he said it had to be up off the collar. So I really cut off three inches too much! But it felt better anyway. Ruthi had to buy a couple of yards of cloth to wrap around her after rolling up her jeans because women don't wear pants in Malawi, and she wouldn't be allowed in looking like the vagabond she was.

The bus dropped us in Chitipa where we slept on the grass outside the rest house, which was closed—no food available. Next morning, another mad bus ride with two stops for major repairs along the way to Nkhata Bay.

In my journal, I wrote that the people of Malawi are friendlier and kinder/gentler than others in East Africa. This contrasts with the repressive police state atmosphere from the officials. Everyone speaks English or tries to and wants to engage us in conversation (Malawi was a British Colony until about twenty years ago). Even during the long waits for the bus to be repaired, we had an enjoyable time talking to our traveling companions. In Nkhata Bay, we spent a day waiting for the ship to arrive to take us down the lake. Lake Malawi is very long, maybe 350 miles. Nkhata Bay is halfway down the lake, where we boarded the good ship *Chauncy Maples*. It is a seagoing vessel built out of parts and used on this inland lake.

Our tickets on the *Chauncy Maples* were for third-class passage, which meant hard benches. Our only hope for sleep was no rain so we could put our bedrolls out on the top of the cabins and sleep outside. We were okay until about 1:00 a.m., when it started to pour. We stole up to the second-class lounge and crashed there the rest of the night.

In the morning, it was still stormy, and I wrote in my journal that as I stood in line for tea, a big wave came over the side and drenched me. It seemed everyone on board, including Ruthi and our traveling companion Owen, were seasick—everyone but me. I just went up as far as I could get on the boat and waited it out.

About noon, we pulled into a bay, and it was like something straight out of a South Seas story. The coconut palms were poking their branches up above the green cove with a nice beach and beautiful green water. The dinghy was dispatched to discharge and bring passengers and cargo onto the *Chauncy Maples*. The village was only visible through the jungle, as we could see the tops of the thatched-roof houses. As we pulled away from the bay, the people picked up their loads of cargo and staggered off down the beach like ants marching away.

Later, we stopped for the night at Nkhotakota Bay, which was billed on the Malawi tourist map as "the largest traditional African village in Southern Africa." We took the dinghy to the beach and jumped off. Unfortunately, Ruthi waited just a little longer than we did and ended up hip deep in water. She shivered the rest of the night. In our travels, we had already seen several traditional villages, and this one didn't seem of much interest to us, and failing to find something to eat, we went back to the boat for the night.

Our destination on the *Chauncy Maples* was Chipoka. We found a place at the rest house there and then arranged for train travel the next day to Blantyre, capital of Malawi. Once again, we had trouble finding something to eat until a little old lady led us down a dusty street to a small mud hut, where she served us *sima* and beans. *Sima* is a mushy, sticky paste made of corn with the consistency of wallpaper paste and tasting only a little better. But we gagged it down because we were so hungry.

Unfortunately, it was so dark and smoky in the hut, I stepped in a hole and turned my ankle so badly, I thought I was going to throw up. It hurt so badly. Next morning, we were hassled by the rest house manager and almost missed the train. It had started to move when we were still fifty yards away. With my swollen ankle, I was prepared to let it go. Thankfully, the conductor saw Ruthi struggling to make it after it had started to move and stopped it for us.

After twelve hours of sitting on hard railway car benches, we finally arrived in Blantyre. The string of towns we passed seemed like they were right out of a Disneyland adventure ride: Gomboliboli, Mtakitaki, Penga Penga, Bilila, and Nankunu. At each town, the train stopped very briefly, and people outside would try to sell food to people inside. The stops were so brief that the people selling food would have to run alongside the train with lots of shouting and passing money and food back and forth.

When we arrived in Blantyre, I helped a lady with two kids and fifty-pound sacks of corn off the train. We left her staring after us on the platform. *What are these foreigners doing here*, she seemed to be thinking.

Blantyre, principal city and capital of Malawi—modern streets, tall buildings, modern, well-stocked shelves in the stores, up-to-date bookshops; what a contrast to the rest of rural Malawi. We wandered around town, taking care of errands, and then spent a few days there waiting for visas and searching out good, cheap places to eat. We found a Chinese restaurant, where we had a good dinner finally after days of starving. Interestingly, most major cities in Africa have good Chinese food—go figure. The rest house was a modern facility too, with a good little restaurant with a menu that reads like other African menus: "Special cocoa, General cocoa, Eggs and toast (one egg), Eggs and toast (two eggs), special rice, local rice."

Because of the civil war in Mozambique, we were advised to take the train from Blantyre to Beira on the coast. It was overcrowded and a difficult trip. At the border, they detached the baggage car and one of the passenger cars, and everyone had to squeeze into the other cars. We went through immigration and customs on the Malawi side, and then everything changed as we entered Mozambique. The immigration and customs guys were all white Portuguese, and they treated us with some deference. They treated the Africans very badly. It was easy to see why the local people hated the colonialists. I buddied up to one of the conductors, who invited Ruthi and me to join him in the caboose. It had soft seats and lots of room for them and us, so we traveled in relative luxury the rest of the way to Beira.

I want to back up and talk about the people on the train. I know I have said that I was doing this for the experience, and being among the people is part of that. But the stench in that third-class railcar with people crammed together after standing in the rain for an hour was unbearable. Most of these people were traveling from Malawi to South Africa to work in the mines. There was even a guard from the Malawi Department of Labor accompanying the laborers who were going to the mines to work. It was a typical African scene, with these people *voluntarily* going to South Africa to work. We didn't understand why they needed a guard.

The train stopped in Dondo to discharge the passengers going to Beira before continuing to Salisbury. We got off the Salisbury train and were going down the platform to the Beira train when it started to leave. We ran to catch it, and Ruthi and I made it, but Owen lost a flip-flop. He stopped to pick it up, and that was just enough delay to make him *really* run and then dive to catch the steps. At last, he pulled himself up on the platform and the conductor let him in.

Later, it was very comical to recall, but he didn't like us laughing at the time. The conductor pronounced that our tickets to Beira were only good on the train we got off, not this one. We tried to explain that that train was not going to Beira but to Salisbury, so how were we supposed to use the tickets on that train. He didn't care and wanted us to pay again. We pled ignorance and poverty and won out in the end but not before some substantial wrangling.

On arrival in Beira, we learned that Estoril is the name of the beach and campground where we could most economically stay. On the way there, I was in culture shock. Estoril is a nice place, and driving through Beira to get there was even more of a shock. Beira is a big European, Mediterranean-like city: miniskirts, modern buildings and streets, see-through blouses, and a horde of lovely Latin-looking chicks being pursued by a horde of young Latin lovers.

At Estoril, the contrast from Africa to Europe was even more pronounced. There was an all-white band playing rock and roll, all white dancers dancing rock and roll, and if it weren't for the black busboys and cooks, I'd have lost perspective altogether. This place is a beach resort for white Rhodesians on holiday. There is no apartheid in Mozambique by law, but here, it seemed as if there was. Culture and economics imposed it since the Africans couldn't afford to come here anyway. Rhodesia is English, and in their own subtly racist way, they avoid being around the blacks.

We found a place in the campground to crash, and then the next morning, we had a shower, some breakfast, and stashed our things in a bungalow before exploring Estoril and Beira. I wasn't impressed with Beira as a town, typical seaside town devoted to the tourists. Estoril was also not interesting to me because the visitors there were mostly racists from Rhodesia, and everything there was set up to keep the blacks out.

We got away from Beira hitching south toward Lorenzo Marques, the capital of Mozambique. A Frenchman picked us up just outside of Beira after we said our goodbyes to Owen, who was going to hitch on his own. The Frenchman worked at a sugar plantation near Dondo, which wasn't all that far from Beira, but on the way there, he convinced us to come with him for a tour of the sugar factory and plantation.

A wealthy Portuguese man, who bought 2,400 acres of land, started the plantation four years before. He then sold a share on credit to each of fifty Portuguese farmers. Each farmer got a farm, a house, a Land Rover, and farming equipment. Now, four years later, all the farmers have paid off their loans for their farms, and the sugar factory has doubled production twice. It's easy to see why the Portuguese want to hold on to this country when you see the level of investment and productivity they are pulling out of it. The Frenchman took us to the plant town and bought us some sandwiches before putting us back out on the highway.

A sugar farmer picked us up and took us about forty kilometers with another stop for sandwiches and drinks along the way. He dropped us off, and after about thirty minutes, a truck came by with Owen in it, and he shouted for the driver to stop. It was funny because usually, when you're hitchhiking, you are at the mercy of your driver, but here was Owen treating the driver like *his* driver! We all piled in, and away we went again for the Lorenzo Marques turnoff.

Arriving there, we walked across the road and had no sooner put our bags down than another guy drove up and said he could take only two. Since there was another couple standing there already, they were loading their stuff when he changed his mind and invited us all to come in with a couple of us riding in the back of his truck. He took us to his store, which was off the road a way and fed us again, then took us back out to the highway to wait for a ride.

At 6:00 p.m., he came back to see if we had gotten a ride. We'd had no luck, so we all piled back into his truck, and he took us home with him for the night. He spoke no English but understood Spanish, which Ruthi knew, so we communicated that way.

The next morning, he took us back out to the highway and then another two hundred kilometers down the road. A nice guy, but at the end, he dumped us off far away from the main road. We managed to get a tourist to take us back to the main road, and then a truck picked us up and took us three hundred kilometers to Maxixe. He dropped us off at a hotel, where we were able to all crowd into one room for not very much money.

Next morning, we went to the edge of town and waited from 6:30 a.m. till 9:00 without anyone picking us up. It was drizzly raining, and I had a slight cold and didn't feel like standing in the rain anymore, so we flagged down a luxury bus, and for four dollars, we traveled all the way to Lorenzo Marques, four hundred kilometers away.

We were not prepared for Lorenzo Marques at all; we had never met anyone who had been there or stayed there. So the bus people gave us the name of the Universal Hotel, where after an argument about how much to pay, we managed to get a room and a meal. Lorenzo Marques was just another European-style city without much to interest us, and we were ready to get to South Africa. Another reason for our haste was the visas we had gotten in Blantyre, Malawi, were only good for a few days, so we were hurrying to get out of Mozambique before the visas expired.

We caught three quick rides to the border of Swaziland and out of Mozambique without any hassle about the visas. On the Swazi side, a South African picked us up and took us to the capital, Mbabane, where all the casinos were. We stashed our bags behind the counter at a grocery store and started exploring Mbabane. Suddenly, it hit me: here I was on the verge of entering South Africa after five months of travel from the northernmost point on the African continent in Alexandria, Egypt. I was excited!

We went to the post office and got mail, which I had been expecting. I had hoped that news of being accepted to a couple of graduate schools the following September would make me happy, but I only felt more confusion. I still was unsettled about what I wanted to do with my life or where or with whom. At that time, I was enjoying the vagabond lifestyle, but it was somewhat hollow after a while; it seemed aimless to me, without a sense of purpose. The acceptance to grad school solved an immediate question of what I'd do next, but for me, it was only a temporary solution to a long-term question.

We looked for a hotel, but they all seemed too expensive to us, so we went out to a campground near the casinos, where we stayed for fifty cents each. We met some South Africans, Derek and Steve, who were very nice and friendly. But we noticed that first, they brought up the subject of apartheid and wanted to talk about it, and second, they seemed perfectly logical, reasonable folks until that subject was introduced. Then they became the most ridiculously narrow-minded people I'd ever met. Ruthi and I talked about how to handle the apartheid issue between us. And we were hoping to avoid it—after all, the US had its own racial problems, and we felt like we lived in a glass house when it comes to criticizing another country's racial problems. But everyone we met brought it up and wanted to talk about it.

It was like they desperately needed our approval for what they were doing and wouldn't shut up until they got it.

Sunday (the day it was easiest to cross into South Africa) was a day away, so we had a day to kill in Mbabane. The city was very modern by African standards and much more so than even Beira or Lorenzo Marques. We looked around the shops and talked to a few more people and learned something about Swaziland. The king here has been the longest reigning king in Africa. He recently disbanded his parliament and put his opposition leader in prison. Once again, we hear the same story: just like Haile Selassie in Ethiopia, Kenyatta in Kenya, Nyerere in Tanzania, and Banda in Malawi—presidents for life!

CHAPTER 13

The sign said, "Nie Blanks" (whites only)

On Sunday, we hitched to the border and had our first taste of apartheid. There were three doors: white, Asian, and nonwhite. We approached the immigration post, fearful of being found out without tickets back home (we'd been told that to enter South Africa, we needed airline tickets back home because they were tired of repatriating hippies). But the intelligence we had heard was very good (that the border crossing on Sundays was chaotic and easy), and they were so busy, they just stamped our passports and visas and passed us quickly through without even asking about our fake tickets.

We caught a ride from the border to Jan Smuts Airport in Johannesburg. Once again, like all the days before, we had incredible luck hitching, and I'm completely convinced it's because we are two clean-cut-looking Americans, a boy and girl, hitching together. It's not safe for a woman to hitch alone, and a guy hitching alone could be trouble—two guys, even more so. Ruthi wanted to ship some junk she'd bought home by air, so while she was doing that, I got on the phone and tried to find my friend Peter Kaal.

Peter and I had been teammates at OSU on the track team. He was from Pretoria, South Africa, about thirty miles north of Jo'burg. He had come to OSU from there in 1966, at the end of my sophomore year there. He was the first South African under eighteen to run the mile in under four minutes. Then that was a big deal. Running under four minutes was still rare, and Jim Ryan, who blew the record apart the following year, had not yet become famous. So getting Peter to come to OSU was a big coup for our coach. We became friends there and kept in touch. I told him I would one day come and see him, and here I was. I reached his mother, who said he was returning that day from a track meet in Luanda, Angola, another Portuguese colony on the other side of Africa. Our trip was about to change again to another direction altogether.

Arriving in Pretoria, we met the parents and Peter's sister. Peter was due back the following day, so they invited us to stay with them and await his arrival. Our first day in Pretoria was both disturbing and interesting: disturbing because of all the overt racism; interesting because it was the most modern European city we'd seen. The Kaals were Afrikanse. White South Africans come from basically two groups: (1) the Afrikaners of basically Dutch ancestry, who first immigrated to that part of South Africa in the late 1700s, and (2) the English, who were close behind the Afrikaners in arriving there. They both claimed that when they arrived in what is now South Africa, it was a barren, empty place. After they began to develop it, they claim the African tribes from the north began to come down to take advantage of this land of milk and honey they created. Of course, the native Africans have a slightly different version of that story.

Afrikaners were the people who were the working class and farmers. The English were the merchants and high-finance business guys. The Afrikaners also controlled the government and did the dirty work of keeping the blacks in line while the English sat back and raked in the money, exploiting both other groups. Once again, this proved my evolving theory of racism and prejudice.

As I mentioned in a previous chapter, the color of prejudice is green, as in money. Prejudice comes from the fear people have of someone else threatening their livelihood. The way that played out in South Africa was that the Afrikaners, who occupy the lowest-paying jobs and level in the society, treated the black people as subhuman. They called them kaffirs, which was similar to the N-word used in the US, except kaffir is more derogatory. It connotes subhuman tribe that is incapable of mixing or assimilating in a modern society.

The Afrikaners instituted the policy of apartheid, separation of the races. Blacks were not allowed to live in the same towns as whites. In fact, while we were there, we heard sirens and whistles at sundown that signaled all black people to be out of town or in their servant living quarters. They were totally excluded from participating in the white society, except in servant roles. There were signs on toilets, banks, post offices, etc., that said, “Nie Blanke” (white only).

If you could look beyond the racism, Pretoria was a very nice town—wide avenues, homes with well-kept lawns, late-model American cars in the driveways, modern buildings. We spent our first day there trying to find Ruthi an inexpensive flight home. She wanted to fly back through London, pick up Suzy her sister, and then fly back to Oregon. She finally found a fare she could live with and booked a flight out on the twenty-first of May, two weeks away. At that point, we both acknowledged that our trip together was coming to an end.

We went to the American Embassy to inquire about visa extensions, and the lady at the desk said, “Oh, yes, Mr. Burrus, she’s expecting you.” That surprised me greatly because I didn’t know anyone was aware of my presence in South Africa other than a few people and certainly not someone at the American Embassy. Well, on that day, a message had come through about me because in Nairobi, I had asked to extend the validity of my passport, which was due to expire. I had told them I would check in with the embassy in South Africa but had forgotten all about that conversation. So when the lady said she was expecting me, I was shocked. While extending my passport, they stamped “US Embassy, Johannesburg” on it. I may have trouble traveling back through the African countries again.

After buying some leather to make another passport case to replace the stolen one in Tanzania, we went back to the Kaals’ house. Peter arrived for dinner and was more than a little surprised to find us there. It was a nice reunion. We talked until late and caught up with each other. Peter had continued competing after he left OSU and had just returned from a major meet, competing for his club in Johannesburg. We agreed to meet the following day in Johannesburg after he got off work.

Riding the bus to Johannesburg the next day, I was struck by the fact that if I was unaware there was a *problem* in South Africa, I'd probably never know. They have worked hard to make the *problem* invisible, except to the most discerning eye. No blacks on the bus or anywhere to be seen. We went to the top of the Carlton Center, tallest building in South Africa, and saw a panorama of the city. There were mine dumps on the edge of the city all around, which had thousands of dollars in gold dust in them. We were told that it would not be worth the effort to try and reclaim the gold from the dumps, but it was an interesting fact. Another interesting fact: I stepped on a scale downtown, and it read seventy-two kilograms, which is right at 159 pounds, the least I've weighed since high school. I guess all the travel and deprivation of the past several months made me leaner.

Peter is not happy here. He misses his girlfriend and life in the US. The only thing keeping him here is his parents, who desperately want him to stay. He is still training hard and competing while trying to hold down a full-time job. If he were in the same situation today, he'd probably find a sponsor to pay him to run; back then, they didn't exist.

One thing I noticed about this white culture: physical fitness seemed very important and runners were everywhere. It's amazing how many people of all ages and both sexes who are active and fit here.

After returning to Pretoria, Ruthi and I decided to take a tour of South Africa before she goes home. We hitchhiked to Durban very quickly and easily as a start. We looked around there, and I left my name at the yacht club in hopes of catching on as a crewman on a sailing vessel going either to Asia or back to the US. Our rides so far (and this would remain true throughout South Africa) have been with Afrikaner policemen or blue-collar types, colored (Indian) businessmen, or the occasional black.

The Afrikaners immediately bring up the issue of race and argue to convince us that first, they are not racists at all, and second, we should accept their point of view that the Bantu (official name for blacks) belong in reserves, separate from the whites. I decided before I got here that I should just listen to their point of view and accept that it is different from mine. It's becoming increasingly difficult, though, to keep my mouth shut in the face of this blatant racism. I also decided that when I couldn't keep quiet, I needed to leave. This is their country, and I would/could never change it, so when I can't accept it, it's bye-bye.

We were driven past several Bantu Township areas, where the blacks have been forced to live far out of town from the whites. They live in simple round mud construction huts called rondavels with thatched roofs. We were able to stay in one, which was part of a motel along the way. The blacks are forced to live apart from the whites, but of course, the only jobs they can get are in the white areas, and they must pay about ten percent of their incomes to travel back and forth.

We learned that there is no television in South Africa, not for any technological reason but for political reasons. Once again, the whites fear giving access to this technology to everyone. If the Bantu can watch modern TV and become enlightened about what's happening around the world, they might not be prepared to just lie down and accept the apartheid. After all, they outnumber the whites, five to one.

The route from Durban to Cape Town is called the Garden Route because it is so beautiful, and we agreed. We traveled from Durban to East London, where we spent the night in a campground under the stars and then on to Port Elizabeth. On the way to Port Elizabeth, a couple of English guys picked us up and told us this joke:

> The British are comprised of four kinds of people: the Scots who keep the Sabbath holy and their pockets full, the Welsh who pray on their knees and on their friends, the Irish who don't know what they believe in but are always willing to die for it, and the English who think they are self-made men and thereby relieving God of the dreadful responsibility.

The English guys were fun loving, drove one hundred miles per hour and talked just as fast all the way to Port Elizabeth. The next ride we caught was with a schoolteacher going to Cape Town. We spent one night in Mossel Bay, where we camped out on the beach in a deserted beach house. The teacher stayed with us, and we talked about the *problem*, and he had some insight on it: the blacks and whites are trapped in a cycle of oppression that will be difficult to break. If the whites allow the blacks to develop a middle class, it may just allow for a transition from apartheid to something else, and the "something else" may not happen without violence and bloodshed, and the whites may not like the result. This development of a middle class would also be an admission by the whites that the blacks can be civilized, which they are loath to admit.

We awoke to a beautiful sunrise on the Indian Ocean. Ruthi took lots of pictures (she has the mind of an artist, and looking at things through her eyes gives me an insight into the beauty of places and things I would never have seen on my own). We traveled on to Cape Town from Mossel Bay, driving through Strand where there were beautiful beaches and through rolling hills along the way. We found a cheap bed-and-breakfast place, the Woodville, in the center of Cape Town and then took the cable car to the top of Table Mountain, the most prominent landmark in Cape Town. From there, we watched the sunset on the Atlantic Ocean and realized that in that same day, we had watched the sunrise and sunset on different oceans.

On top of Table Mountain, we met some nice guys who agreed to drive us to an area where there were cheap and good restaurants. In the end, they decided to accompany us there. After that, we went to a beer hall and drank with them until late, and they finally dropped us at the B and B.

The next couple of days we rented a car and drove out to the end of the Cape, the south end of the continent. Then we drove to Stellenbosch to visit the wineries and sample some of the local fare. We toured a winery and bought some wine to bring back to the Kaals for being so nice to us. Cape Town is the most liberal of all South Africa, with more mixing of races, but it's still South Africa. In appearance, Cape Town reminded me a little of San Francisco.

On the sixteenth of May, we left Cape Town early in the morning, intending to hitchhike back through the Klein Karoo and the Great Karoo (desert areas that look like West Texas or Arizona) to Jo'burg. It took us seven rides to go from Cape Town to Oudtshoorn, a small country town with very friendly smiling people all around. Just outside of Oudtshoorn is the Cango Caves, much like the Carlsbad Caverns. On the tour, it was necessary in a couple of places to shinny through spaces only wide enough if you held your breath and crawling on our belly through a space between the rocks. It was so narrow, we couldn't even get on our knees, and when I breathed deeply, my back and chest both touched the walls—a little too claustrophobic for Ruthi (me too, but I wouldn't admit it).

After the caves, we started hitching north and had the worst day of hitching ever. The last ride dropped us off in the middle of nowhere, about fifty miles from the nearest town. He turned off onto a dirt road and waved goodbye at 3:30 p.m., and that was that. We waited until dusk with no luck. I walked down the road and up to a farmhouse and asked if we could put our bedrolls down on the grass just inside his compound to avoid being eaten by the wildlife. The lady listened to us and then went and got her husband, who also listened to us, and just about the time I thought he was going to throw us off his property, he smiled and invited us in.

He turned out to be an amateur archeologist in his spare time and a farmer by vocation. He had built a small museum behind his house, where he had displayed the fossils and bones of animals and men from millions (?) of years ago. These people had grown children and had obviously been starved for much social interaction for a long time, so after dinner, we broke out a bottle of the Stellenbosch wine we brought and sat and talked for hours.

Next morning, we resisted their invitation to stay until the weekend when their kids were coming home, and they were all going springbok (small deer) hunting. These people were very, very nice and generous, like many of the South Africans we met. However, when "the problem" came up, they became the most bullheaded, narrow minded, irrational people I'd ever met. Even if they recognized all this, they were caught in a situation not of their making, and they had no choice but to hold the line. They also genuinely believed that they were there first'; they had ancestors four generations back who had hacked out an existence here. They saw themselves as just as much *African* as the blackest man there. I could see their situation, but they could not and would not allow even the slightest acceptance of how wrong the apartheid policy was.

After we said our goodbyes to these nice people, we went out to the road, and the second car passing picked us up. A few very fast-driving rides later, we had raced through Bloemfontein, capital of the Orange Free State, where they are most oppressive to the Bantu, to a small town of Wynberg. All along the way since leaving Cape Town, we have seen ostrich farm after ostrich farm. In those days, it was before any ostrich had been imported into the US, so seeing them was a real treat.

Finally, on the nineteenth of May, we were back to Johannesburg. Ruthi was in a hurry to get back there to get her mail, and when she looked in her bag for her wallet, it was gone, including her passport. This was a big problem for her because she was planning to catch a plane in just two days. We went to the embassy, and she managed to sweet-talk them into giving her a replacement passport, which was a little more difficult because it was the second one she had lost in Africa in the past four months. So after a lecture from an embassy official, she got her replacement passport, and we returned via bus to Pretoria.

Our last ride was interesting. We were standing on the side of the road in a residential area, and a man parked his car in front of us. As he walked toward his front door, he asked where we were going. After a short conversation, he got back in his car and drove us there. But it was only after we got in the car that we smelled the booze; he was smashed! Somehow, he managed to drive us safely to the Kaals' house, and when we got out, he said tearily, "I only hope the rest of the world treats you as nice as me!" A hitchhiker's life is never dull!

This brings me to the end of another chapter—1,660 miles of hitchhiking through South Africa in two weeks. In total, 5,600 miles of travel by hitch, bus, train, ship, and truck from Nairobi with Ruthi, including the trip to Mombasa and Lamu. She had teared up several times in the last few days, sad because our time together was nearing an end. I was sad too; she is a lovely young woman and a joy to travel with. I could even see the potential of a future with her. However, she was ready to leave and move on with her life.

It made me sad, continuing my journey without her, so my anxiety was doubled by the loss of my traveling companion and the prospect of having to make it the rest of the way on my own. I was down to a small-enough sum of money that I simply couldn't do what she did and just buy a ticket home. If I borrowed going-home money from my parents, I'd never hear the end of it, so I was determined to do it myself.

I considered staying in South Africa to work for a while. In good conscience, I decided I couldn't support the apartheid by staying and working there. I didn't have enough money or desire to try and carry on traveling through India (I had been told by people coming from India that it was pretty bleak), so the decision was made: I would get back to the US and get into a graduate school to become legitimate again (American businesses didn't hire hippies) and then see what happened next.

CHAPTER 14

Homeward Bound

No, you may not sleep here! You're going to jail

It was time for Ruthi to leave. We got her stuff together, took her to the airport, and after some tearful goodbyes, she left; and suddenly, it was all over. The travel through Africa instantly ended for me. I couldn't fly home from Jo'burg because I didn't have enough for a ticket, so the only thing remaining is to backtrack to Nairobi and fly home. That's the way I felt anyway—just finished.

At this point in the summer of 1973, all I wanted to do was get home. I was nearly broke financially, and losing Ruthi as a companion was working on my head. I was looking forward to some stability back home. I didn't know how I would achieve that stability or where or with whom, but I longed for it.

After Ruthi left, I went into Jo'burg with Peter and spent a few days before going for a weekend trip to the mountains. Peter was still training hard, and he took me to his club, the Wanderers Club. It is supposedly the biggest and best-furnished club of its kind in the world. I didn't doubt it. Every sport you could imagine was available including two golf courses, indoor and outdoor tennis, indoor and outdoor Olympic sized swimming pools, state-of-the-art running tracks, etc. I tried to keep up with Peter on a couple of his runs and could do so for a couple of miles, but then his conditioning wiped me out, and I had to walk.

I spent a few more days with Peter before heading north. We traveled to places with names like Magoebese Kloof, Debengeni Falls, Tzaneen, God's Window, Graskop, and Pilgrim's Rest. This was the heart of the gold region where they first found it in South Africa. There were lots of stories about the success and romance of the early gold fields.

Then after a nice, long visit to South Africa, it was time to go. There was tension with the Kaals; they feared I would influence Peter to leave. So Peter took me out to the highway, and I was off on my hitchhiking trip again. After several quick rides, I found myself crossing the Limpopo River into Southern Rhodesia. At a crossroad, one road went to Bulawayo and Victoria Falls; the other went to the capital, Salisbury. I stood on the side of the road, basically prepared to go whichever way the first car stopping to pick me up was going.

After several hours and getting dark, a policeman came along and suggested that instead of being consumed by a lion, I might like to sleep in his jail. So he took me to jail, and again, I had a first experience: I had never and have not since spent the night in a jail. But he left the door open, and there were no other inmates that I can remember, so I had a pretty good night's sleep. That is, until a little wizened old black man with a broom about fifteen inches long came in and noisily began to sweep up at 6:00 a.m.

Over that night, I decided I would be crazy to spend all that time in Africa and not see Victoria Falls, so I left the jail committed to getting a ride up there. I was just sure that my bad hitching luck of the previous day would change. I waited until 10:00 a.m., and after several cars stopped to ask if I was *sure* I didn't want to go to Salisbury, a funny little man named Rader in a big truck stopped to pick me up. He had huge blue-colored glasses, which looked like they probably belonged to his wife, and a wide flat smile. He worked for the Wankie Colliery and was returning there with a truckload of spare parts for the coal mining machinery.

I rode with him from 10:00 a.m. to after 7:00 p.m., 420 miles. Along the way, he stopped several times for six packs of Castle beer (I lost count after three), and we arrived at his house in Wankie sloshed. His wife, a frumpy little lady with a take-charge attitude and another wide grin, herded us into the house and into a couple of hot baths, just like she'd done this many times before.

After a quick dinner, he took me to the Colliery Club number 1, which was more nicely appointed than any officers' club I'd seen. Everything in Wankie is owned, operated, and/or sanctioned by the coal mining company. Of course, all the people at the club are white—managers and clerical types. The blacks do the real work of mining. I got a little glimpse into their life—not for me but very interesting.

The last day of May 1973, my bag ripped. I had reduced my stuff I carried around to a small fifteen-inches-in-diameter-by-twenty-four-inch-long canvas bag and sleeping bag. The canvas bag that carried everything in it split right down the middle along the zipper—unrepairable. Now it was really time to go home! I managed to hold it together by tying leather thongs around it in four places.

The Raders tried to get me to stay a few days more with them. I'm beginning to believe the stories I'd heard about how kind and generous the Rhodesians are compared to the South Africans. But I was determined to keep heading for home, so I said my goodbyes and headed out to the highway. A policeman picked me up and took me not just to the highway but to the best place on the highway to catch a ride. One of the first cars passing picked me up.

That's how I met Jake and Lorraine. I didn't write much in my journal about her, except that she was stunningly beautiful and young enough to be his daughter. I wrote a lot about him. He's a white South African by passport but a Scotsman through and through. In his short forty-ish, life he's been a professional hunter, a taxidermist, archeologist, geologist, and is presently doing consulting work for the Queen Victoria Museum in Salisbury. He can do a perfect imitation of an Indian-speaking English and can swear in six languages, including Hindi.

As we approached the Victoria Falls, we could see the spray of water mushrooming into the sky five miles away. We drove down and parked near the falls and walked to within fifty meters. That close to one of the biggest falls in the world, it's a rain forest. It rains from every direction and up and down. No amount of rain gear will help. It's the kind of experience you can't photograph or even explain properly. It's awe-inspiring to see multiple rainbows every direction you look. The Africans have a word for Victoria Falls that means "big smoke that roars." It was humbling.

I had dinner at the Victoria Falls Hotel with Jake and Lorraine, and we laughed at Jake's Scottish reaction to the falls: he wanted to dig under it and get all the gold deposited there. They dropped me at the campground for the night.

I thought about crossing over from Rhodesia to Zambia at the falls and traveling up through Zambia toward my destination, Nairobi. I had learned that it was very difficult to get across the border between Rhodesia and Zambia. They were technically at war, but the result for tourists was to make it virtually impossible to cross the bridge over the Zambezi River. So I bought a cheap airline ticket from Salisbury to Dar es Salaam in Tanzania, which was departing in a couple of days. After seeing Rhodesia and meeting so many nice people, I was sorry to be hurrying through the country.

I met a girl who worked at a tourist office who helped me get tickets on the train and a discounted ticket for a plane ride over the falls and the game parks nearby. Seeing the falls from above was just as spectacular as being close to it, maybe more so.

After the plane ride, I met some other travelers who encouraged me to stay there that night and hitch to Bulawayo the following day and catch the overnight train from there to Salisbury. I wanted to see some African dances at the big hotel but got thrown out because I didn't have long pants on (actually, I didn't own any). Back at the campground, after the usual campfire conversation, I crashed for the night, hoping to get up in time to see the sunrise over the falls.

Next morning, after a good hot bath at the campground, I walked out to the road and watched the sunrise waiting for a ride. One of the first cars passing picked me up. The driver, Martin, was a very interesting guy. He was from Cape Town and working for a bank when he met this nice Jewish girl from Bulawayo, Rhodesia. He swept her off her feet, and a few weeks later, she sent him a ticket to come to Bulawayo for the weekend. Turns out, she's the only child of the owners of the biggest ranch (350,000 acres, eighty thousand head of cattle) in Rhodesia. His three-day weekend turned into ten days, and he went home engaged to the daughter. They were desperate to find a nice Jewish boy for her.

Martin was six feet six inches and 270 pounds and an imposing character. He said to me, "That girl loves me and has more money than she knows what to do with. It's an opportunity I can't pass up. I can learn to love her." So he entered the relationship a glorified stud to sire an heir to the family fortune and never looked back.

He bought my lunch at the Wankie Game Reserve Lodge (when a guy that size says, "I'll buy your lunch," he does, and that's that). He took me to the train station, and as I was stewing over whether to buy a second- or third-class ticket, he pushed me out of the way and bought me a first-class ticket. Turning to me, he had this mischievous grin on his face and said, "I'll just pay for first-class and charge it to the ranch, ha ha!"

I had some time to kill before the overnight train and wandered around Bulawayo. I met yet another nice Rhodesian, Steve, an agricultural economics student at Salisbury University. He too tried to talk me out of leaving Rhodesia in such a hurry and told me about some fantastic things to see and do using Salisbury as a base. As I look back on it now, I am kicking myself for the all-fired hurry I was in to get back to Nairobi and home, but it's hard to remember at this point just how I felt about getting home after being on the road for fifteen months (and how broke I was).

The plane was leaving at 9:00 a.m. from Salisbury, and the train from Bulawayo did not arrive until 8:00 a.m., so I decided to leave it up to fate: if I could make the connection I would go; if not, I'd stay and catch the same flight the following week. I jumped off the train as it was coming to a stop, and with my light load, I beat the crowd to the curb and caught the first cab to the airport. The next thing I knew, I was taking off from Salisbury Airport toward Dar es Salaam with a stop in Blantyre en route. While in the air, I decided to save the sixty-five dollars it cost to go on from Blantyre to Dar es Salaam, and so I got off the plane in Blantyre and got my money back.

I had to get Zambian and Kenyan visas in Blantyre, so I was stuck there a couple of days. What a drag! After the efficiency of

Rhodesia, being back in black Africa was tedious. I met a couple named Bruce and Sandi at the Blantyre Rest House. At a restaurant, he convinced the waiter that we couldn't wear ties for religious reasons (and the guy bought it). He had a line of blarney a mile long.

I wanted to get to Monkey Bay at the southern end of Lake Malawi, so I could catch the *Chauncy Maples* again. So early on the fifth of June, I headed for the highway. A couple of quick rides dropped me at the Monkey Bay turnoff, and there I sat for several hours. Finally, a Caterpillar 12G Motor Grader came lumbering along, and I held out my thumb in jest. To my surprise, the Portuguese machinery operator stopped, and to my greater surprise, he had me driving within a few miles! He hung out on the side of the grader and laughed, "Caught a ride on a bloody grader, didn't you? Ha ha."

After forty miles and two hours on a dusty road grader, I was ready for a less adventurous ride. In the little town of Mangochi, I was looking for the bus station when I met Christopher-Hensley, *mtoliro* (headmaster) of the Mangochi Secondary School. He insisted on being my guide around Mangochi, and we had a meal together. He was quite a character.

There were people at the Monkey Bay Campground that I had met on the plane and at the Blantyre Rest House, including Bruce and Sandi. So once again, I found myself with a bunch of vagabond hippies at a campground in Africa. A couple of things happened there worth mentioning. There was a hippopotamus that came up to within fifteen meters of the beach every night. It was a little frightening because she came up so close to where we were camping, but I won a free beer by going out into the water and splashing her before running back to the shelter of the campfire. (I later learned that hippos could run faster than a man—another case of dumb luck.)

The other thing was a walk I took out of Monkey Bay and along the cliffs overlooking it. A dog I had played with the night before joined me, and as we walked, she decided to become my tour guide. When we would come to a fork in the road, she stopped as I took the wrong way and waited for me to return. Then she pranced down the right path, tail wagging, big smile. Once I heard an animal in the bush and whistled for her and pointed. She ran up and barked until whatever it was, was gone and then rejoined the tour. At a lookout point on the cliff, I stopped and sat down to take it in, and she lay down beside me—a good tour guide.

There was a village a little further along, which was only accessible by dirt track or dugout canoe. I thought to myself, *Maybe this will be the time I get to a place where no white men have been before.* When I got there, a big burly Australian came out of a grass-thatched hut with a pile of books and said, "Wanna trade, mate?"

The trip by boat, rented truck, bus, and hitchhiking by car back through Zambia to Dar es Salaam, Tanzania, was tedious but uneventful. Most of the people from Monkey Bay were traveling the same direction, so we used our numbers to bargain for prices for rides along the way. There were three *Geordies*, guys from the northeast of England that speak the Northeast England dialect (unintelligible) that traveled with me and booked into a cheap hotel in Dar es Salaam. They were virtually impossible to understand until we'd all had a few beers. They were pipeline welders whose welds were certified by Lloyd's of London, meaning that when they bury the pipe, they want to make sure that it doesn't leak. They were paid a lot of money to do this, so every few months, they'd make tons of money and then go play for a while. They were between jobs.

One night, the most adventurous of the Geordies disappeared for a while and then came roaring into the hotel at midnight without any pants. He kept shouting, "The bitch stole me pants!" over and over. He had met an African girl and gone to a room with her, and while they were *engaged*, someone reached into the window and stole his pants with wallet and everything in them. A comical moment!

I found Dar es Salaam to be dreary and bleak. It has a decidedly Muslim atmosphere to it, which seems foreign compared to a place like Nairobi. At that time, it was also bleak because Tanzania was one of the poorest countries in Africa. All the stores were empty, and the restaurants were lousy. Time to move on.

I caught a couple of quick rides that took me long distances, and by about 5:00 p.m., I was in Moshi once again at the base of the "big mountain" Kilimanjaro. I was so pleased with my hitchhiking luck that I spent some time writing down what I thought at the time were the cardinal rules of hitchhiking:

- Have faith. You have to believe that someone is going to pick you up. Your lack of faith and fear of not getting a ride comes across in your bearing, your face, and people will not stop for someone with a *problem.*
- Never give up on a ride. If you do give up on getting a ride, the gods of hitchhiking will not favor you with a ride the next time.
- Never refuse a ride no matter how short. By refusing a ride, you are rejecting the good karma of the road.
- The longer you wait for a ride, the better the ride will be in some unexpected way.
- Be straightforward and humble. You must make yourself seen and ask for a ride from every conveyance passing. It's not for you to decide the relative comfort of the ride. Ask from every car or truck passing, and let what happens happen.
- Be relaxed. Aggressiveness won't get you a ride any faster. In fact, it scares people because they don't understand your urgency.
- If you must use a sign, keep it simple and humorous. Often, a sign hurts as much as it helps because people who would have stopped may not be going as far or as short as it says on your sign. Also, the karma of the road decides how far or short you go, not you.

(Looking at what I wrote back then in 1973, it's easy to see that my spiritual journey was evolving. Now I'm convinced that it was the grace of God and not the karmic gods of hitching that got me through that travel experience. This will be evidenced in this next section more clearly.)

In order not to anger the gods of hitching, I did not pursue a bus to Arusha that night but went back out on the road after having a couple of cups of coffee at the YMCA. I waited a long time and after dark (when most people will never pick you up). I was thinking about bedding down by a church across the road when a truck stopped. The entire English vocabulary of the people on this truck was "Okay, let's go." I asked them where they were going, and they replied, "Okay, let's go." I asked them when they would get there and if I could have a ride and always got the same answer: "Okay, let's go."

So I jumped up in the back of the truck, and away we went across the African savannah. After an hour or so, the servant riding in the back with me began asking me in Swahili about my clothes and where I was from. Then he began to ask for money. I told him I didn't have any money, but he wouldn't listen, and he eventually pounded on the roof of the cab, and they stopped. I stayed in the back as the other four of them got down and gathered to talk by the front right tire. I understood the Swahili words for white man and steal and money, all of which were being used. I was afraid. There was nowhere to go; we were in the middle of the Tanzanian wilderness with wild animals all around. Even if I wanted to run away, I couldn't. I was bigger than them but not sure I could take them all.

It was time to put my beliefs about human nature to the test. I believed at the time that you get what you give. If you expect people to rob you, they probably will. If you expect people to help you and be generous to you, you must give them the chance to do it and expect it. So I jumped down out of that truck and walked around to the Muslim driver, who had invited me to join them. I put my arm around him and said (to this man who understood not one word of English) that I thought the tire was just fine. I smiled and shook his hand and then shook the hands of all the others, all the time keeping up my positive banter and trying to get the idea across that I trusted them.

It was quiet for a few seconds, and then the driver gave a command to the others, and they began to get back on the truck; he smiled at me and shook my hand, and I knew things were going to be all right. When we got to Arusha, he dropped the others off and then took me home with him. He gave me a room in his house and then waited while I cleaned up and changed. Then he walked down to the center of the village, holding my hand like a little boy and ordered a plate of goat curry and waited while I ate it. Best plate of goat curry I have ever eaten! He paid for it and then walked me back to his house, which was a mud hut with thatched roof and bid me good night.

At dawn, he got me up and drove me the ten miles back out to the highway, parked his truck so people would have to stop to get around it, and waited there until someone stopped. He referred to me as his friend and asked each driver to take me. What a nice man! From being afraid for my life twelve hours before, I stood there, hugging him and bidding him goodbye. Instead of being robbed in the wilderness, I was befriended and cared for by a very nice Muslim truck driver. My biggest regret is that I did not get his name or contact info. The power of *love* won the day!

I made it across the border into Kenya and back to Nairobi on June 17. There was one minor hassle at the border with another Kenyan border guard giving me a hard time for my appearance, but a kindly English gentleman had a word with him, and they let me pass. With my last few Tanzanian shillings, I bought a small three-legged stool carved from a single tree and a wooden club carved from a baobab tree. I ended up carrying these things back to the US through London and Dublin. Imagine an American with long hair and beard, carrying a small cylindrical canvas bag, tank top, and patched jeans and carrying African wooden art.

Finally, after three months, I was back at City Park, Nairobi. Amazingly, several people I'd met in my travels were also there. I only had two things I wanted to do in Nairobi: (1) get a cheap ticket to London and (2) get a ride up north to the best place to watch the total eclipse of the sun. This was supposed to be the most complete total eclipse of this century, and I didn't want to miss it.

I met some new people at City Park, one of whom was Earl, an American who had a passion to see the source of the Nile. I told him about going to the source of the Blue Nile, the Blue Nile Falls in Ethiopia. We knew that the source of the White Nile was in Uganda, so we began talking about how to get there. We met an Australian guy who also wanted to go and share expenses. Our first visit was to the American Embassy. They said, "Do not go to Uganda." The Idi Amin regime was ruthless and out of control, killing lots of people all over Uganda, and they would not be responsible if we got into trouble there.

Then we went to the British Embassy. There, they told us it was "a bit dicey" and to be careful. Finally, we went to the Australian Embassy. The Aussie we talked to said, "Sure, mate, it's easy. You just take the overnight bus to Kampala, rent a car there, and drive up to Murchison Falls, the source of the White Nile. No problem." We chose to listen to him and not the others.

We made it to the falls easily, and it was interesting but after Victoria Falls, it was not as spectacular for me as for the others. The whole Nile River is forced into a twenty-foot-wide gorge, so it was still spectacular. Also, it was a totally unspoiled and virgin jungle, which added to the mystique. We were charged by a mama elephant when we got in between her and her calf. The reverse gear on that rental car got a good workout!

We had a bit of a problem when we headed back from Murchison Falls. We had been up for thirty-six hours or so, and the guy driving (not me) fell asleep and ran off the road, damaging the car. Africans came out of the bush and helped us pull the fender away from the tire, and we were able to drive back to Kampala, but we worried all the way back about what kind of trouble we'd be in—no insurance. Well, we needn't have worried.

The owner of the rental car company was an Indian guy who was even more desperate to escape from Uganda than the other Indians I'd run into in other countries. When he learned that we had some hard currency—dollars and travelers checks (we emptied our pockets)—he took the money (about 350 dollars) and let us go without another word about the car. We again caught the bus back to Nairobi with only a minor hassle at the border. On the trip back, we passed by Lake Nakuru, where the scene was completely pink—flamingos everywhere, thousands of them.

Back at City Park again, I met some other people who would prove important to me in the days to come. One couple was Mike and Sherry, ex-military types who were traveling around and really wanted to see the eclipse. Another was Ian from the village of Stonehouse in the English Cotswolds. He was also traveling around but getting ready to go home, so I told him I'd try and look him up in England (which I did a couple of weeks later).

The total eclipse was something very hard to describe. We drove north out of Nairobi a couple of hours where the most perfect place was supposed to be. When the eclipse happened, out there in the African bush, it was eerie. There were some giraffes nearby, and when the moon blocked the sun, they knelt on their knees. I'm sure they just thought it was nighttime, but to us, it looked like they were involved in a worship experience. We saw stars above us, but just fifty miles away in the desert, it was light.

Back in Nairobi, I went to the travel agency owned by yet another Indian and bargained for a cheap fare back to London. It took three weeks of bargaining. He kept trying to explain that you couldn't bargain for airfare, and I kept telling him that this was East Africa and you could bargain for everything. I asked if he had seats free on the flight for this Saturday, and he said yes. So I returned on Saturday and asked again, and he said yes but no discount. So I left his store and went to the camera shop and changed some money at twelve to one. Then I went to the airport and changed money for some tourists in brand new safari suits for eight to one. I made four schillings on the dollar, enough to live on for a week.

The following week, I went back and went through the same routine with the Indian travel agent. Finally, after three weeks, success; he discounted the fare for me. Using black market shillings and negotiating the price, I was able to get the ticket. I think the original fare was something like 350 dollars, and I paid about two hundred dollars.

The plane landed at Ostend, Belgium, where we had to clear immigration and customs and then take a hovercraft and bus on to London. Suddenly, the trip was over. Here's what I wrote in my journal:

> I realized as I stepped down off the plane that for the past eight months there had been an apprehension of adventure, of the unknown, of all the feelings associated with 'the bush' just a stone's

> throw out there somewhere. Each day brought new discoveries, unique to me and making my life dynamic. With the landing in Europe came a sickly predictability in place of the apprehension of adventure. Instead of having a feeling of relief of being in civilization, I found it confining, even overwhelming with the speed of life compared to the laidback existence of Africa. I saw the re-entry into western civilization the same as coming into a new kind of jungle—a psychological jungle with predators trying to possess my mind instead of consume my body.

A little melodramatic maybe, but that's the way I felt.

Arriving in England from the comfort of a beautiful tour bus, I noticed a car smash a motorcycle, a car smash another car, a lot of cars stirring dust and fumes in the face of a strawberry salesman on the side of the road. I saw what we'd call today road rage of Sunday drivers stuck in endless traffic jams. I was not pleased to be back in civilization.

I had thought of several places I thought I could stay in London, but none of them panned out. By the time I learned this, it was late in the evening, after flying all day, in culture shock, and my eyes burning from the smog. I was standing next to a park, thinking about bedding down there when a bobby came up to me and gave me a brochure about a "youth camp" just outside of London. It turned out to be the same place I had stayed the previous summer with Gail, but with about one third the people and a little better organized.

I spent a couple of days in London, finding my way for the next and final part of the trip. At a student travel office, I learned that there was a student charter from Dublin to New York for 31.50 pounds sterling (about seventy-five dollars), which sounded the best I'd heard about, so I committed to taking it. At the camp, I met a guy who had just bought a new 650 BSA motorcycle. He had to put five hundred miles on it before he could change the break-in oil; *did*

I have a deal for him. We took off from East Acton Tent City, heading for the Cotswolds, about one hundred miles west of London.

We made it to Ian's house, the guy I had met in Nairobi City Park, by midafternoon. The Cotswolds is a beautiful, picturesque part of England, famous for their stone fences made of white rock. We went to rugby practice with Ian, had a typical English dinner with his family, went down the lane to the village pub, helped a farmer next door put up some hay, and generally had a very nice taste of England. It was my final memory of England for several years, and it was a very good one.

On the fifth of July, Ian dropped me off at the motorway heading north, and by the evening, I had hitched to Liverpool, bought a ticket on the Dublin ferry, and took in a movie before catching the overnight ferry. In Dublin, I made the final arrangements for the flight home: getting the fake student ID, buying the student ticket, and getting to know Dublin a little bit.

The rest of the trip is a blur. I stopped writing in my journal at this point because I think I was in total shock. The flight from Dublin to New York was uneventful, and I don't even remember how I got from the airport in New York to the highway in New Jersey, where I caught a ride and hitched back to Washington, DC. I called my parents from the freeway in Frederick, Maryland, and they came and picked me up, and I was home!

The next day after I got home, Susan Scheffel called from San Francisco. She had just returned from the Philippines and wondered where Raymond was.

CHAPTER 15

Sandstorm

Why is the book called *Son of a Sandstorm*? Because I am the son of Hershel "Sandstorm" Burrus. His full name was Raymond Hershel Burrus. But there is more than one meaning here: Oklahoma was in the heart of the dust bowl during the Great Depression, so I came along right after that terrible time but not so long as to forget the sandstorms, so famous for Western Oklahoma. I am also a son of the generation who survived the Great Depression and a son of the red dirt of Oklahoma that blew throughout my childhood.

Sandstorm and me 1971

Sandstorm's mother died in childbirth when he was five, and after his father got back on his feet and remarried, he took his two kids (my father and his sister, Lou Emma) and his wife's three kids and, with a wagon and team of mules, went to West Texas to start over and homestead some land out there in 1921. The homestead was a mile south and a mile east of Whitharral, Texas (halfway between Levelland and Littlefield).

By the time he was fifteen in 1930, the Great Depression was making life tough. He had missed three years of school, working in the cotton fields, and so having only finished sixth grade, he decided to try and make it on his own. He hitchhiked back to Hollis, Oklahoma, and found lodging in a hotel basement and washed dishes for his keep. Some of the old-timers in the town would hang around the hotel and bait traveling salesmen into a bet. They would tell the traveler that they had an old boy back in the kitchen who could run fast but probably not as fast as someone like them from the big city. Invariably, arrogance and pride would win out, and they would put their money down that they could surely outrun a hick from this little town.

Daddy never lost! By the time he was in high school, he was playing football, basketball, and baseball and running in whatever track meets that were held in that part of the state. He also never lost a race there, set some records, and was the best half miler around. In one race, running on a sandy track, he got out in front, and with his long stride, he kicked sand in the faces of the other runners. After the race, one of them teased him, saying, "Hershel, we felt like we were running in a sandstorm behind you!"

A sportswriter from the newspaper happened to overhear it, and the headline read, "Sandstorm Burrus wins again!." For the rest of his life, he was known as "Sandstorm" Burrus. He went on to set records around the state and caught the attention of legendary track coach Ralph Higgins. Higgins offered him a scholarship to come to Oklahoma A&M (now OSU) and run track.

In those depression days, a scholarship meant he would have a job and be able to work his way through school. He met my mother, Dorothy, who was visiting from Tulsa. With friends, she attended a track meet and was offered a blind date with "that long-legged kid" winning races.

When they both finished school, they married and suffered through World War II. He was a second lieutenant in the infantry, and after recovering from his war injuries, they settled back in Oklahoma, and he became a very successful executive in various agricultural government jobs. He was the first person in his family ever to attend or graduate from college. With his successful career, he was seen as a real hero in the family. And he was certainly a larger-than-life hero to me. In retirement, he played golf every day and could shoot his age in his seventies before his debilitating strokes. He died in 1996 just before his eighty-first birthday.

I have proudly lived in his shadow most of my life. So this book is dedicated to his memory. I am truly the son of a sandstorm: Sandstorm Burrus.

Hershel and Dorothy in 1943, right before he shipped out for Okinawa

Let me also brag on that lady in the picture. At the time of this writing, she is 102. She has a PhD in education and had a very successful career as an educator, author, and administrator, finishing her career in Howard County, Maryland. She has two children, two grandchildren, and six great-grandchildren, who all adore her, now known as "Gigi." She too was the first in her family to graduate from college. She has encouraged me to write this book.

AFTERWORD

That last chapter ended just prior to my twenty-seventh birthday. Susan and I reconnected in San Francisco, and we hitchhiked back to Oklahoma, stopping in Phoenix to check out the graduate school. Susan and I married that summer, and I attended the Thunderbird Graduate School of International Management, graduating in December 1974.

By this time, I was twenty-nine, about six years older than the average student there. I had been an officer with command experience in Vietnam and had traveled in over forty countries. This résumé gave me a leg up with the interviewers, and so I had a choice of seven companies from which to choose. I accepted an offer from Caterpillar Tractor Company, and after eighteen months of training in Peoria, Illinois (they called it "getting the yellow paint in my veins"), I was sent to Hong Kong.

We were in Hong Kong from 1976 to 1986 and had two children there: Elizabeth, born in 1977, and Katherine in 1978. We absolutely loved living in Hong Kong, making many lifelong friends. After a year in Hong Kong, I joined a British group, Inchcape, and continued to manage businesses involved in construction, concrete, and quarrying. It was during the end of our Hong Kong experience that I came back into fellowship and renewed my belief in Jesus Christ. (That's a much longer and involved story that will have to wait for another telling.)

From Hong Kong, we moved to Jakarta, Indonesia, for eighteen months and finally moved back to the US in 1987. I continued to work in heavy and industrial equipment businesses based in Minnesota, Texas, and Oklahoma for the next twenty-five years.

Those businesses still involved substantial overseas travel. At this writing, I have traveled and/or worked in eighty-five countries.

Our daughters attended university in the late '90s, married in 2002, and now have families of their own. We have six grandkids: four granddaughters and two grandsons. We split our time between Bellingham, Washington, and Chicago, where our daughters live. We have a home in Dallas, where my mother, who is 102 at this writing, is still going strong, living independently, and spending time with her close friend Dick, who lives next door.

I could write another book about my experiences during the last thirty-four years, but that will have to wait. This book detailed my life up until age twenty-seven, a very intense and memorable time for me. I hope you enjoyed it.

—Raymond Burrus, August 2021

ABOUT THE AUTHOR

Raymond Burrus is a retired international sales executive, splitting his time between homes in Dallas, Texas, and Bellingham, Washington. He and Susan, his wife of forty-eight years, have two children and six grandchildren. He dotes on those grandkids and sees that as his full-time job now—granddaddy.

He has traveled and/or worked in eighty-five countries. He is originally from Oklahoma, where he grew up and then spent four years as an officer in the US Army.

After the military, he vagabonded twenty-seven countries in Europe and thirteen countries in Africa, mostly hitchhiking. He attended Thunderbird Grad School of International Management and then started his career in international business. In his mind, he's still a vagabond masquerading as a retired sales executive.

He loved living in Hong Kong for ten years and says it's his favorite place, but it has nothing to do with weather or geography. It's all about the wonderful and lifelong friends they made there.

CPSIA information can be obtained
at www.ICGtesting.com
Printed in the USA
LVHW021110210622
721764LV00003B/396